Wakefield Press

The Last Protector

Cameron Raynes teaches history and creative writing at the University of South Australia and is also the author of a collection of short stories (*The Colour of Kerosene*) and a novel (*First Person Shooter*). He lives in Adelaide with his wife and two children.

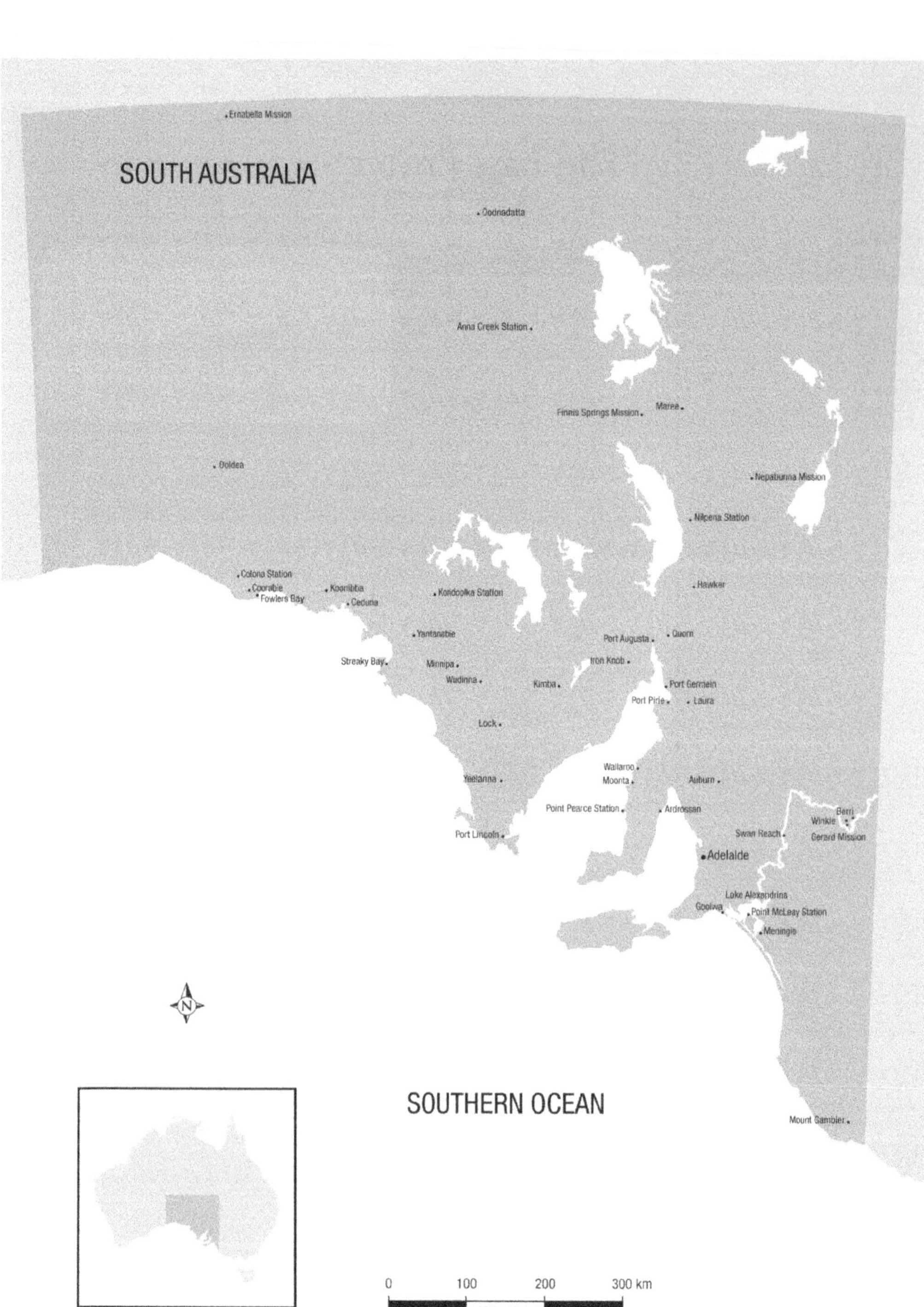
Ernabella Mission
SOUTH AUSTRALIA
Oodnadatta
Anna Creek Station
Finnis Springs Mission
Maree
Ooldea
Nepabunna Mission
Nilpena Station
Colona Station
Coorabie
Fowlers Bay
Koonibba
Ceduna
Kondoolka Station
Hawker
Yantanabie
Port Augusta
Quorn
Streaky Bay
Minnipa
Iron Knob
Wudinna
Kimba
Port Germein
Port Pirie
Laura
Lock
Wallaroo
Moonta
Auburn
Yeelanna
Point Pearce Station
Ardrossan
Berri
Winkie
Port Lincoln
Swan Reach
Gerard Mission
Adelaide
Lake Alexandrina
Goolwa
Point McLeay Station
Meningie
N
SOUTHERN OCEAN
Mount Gambier
0
100
200
300 km

The Last Protector

The illegal removal of Aboriginal children from their parents in South Australia

Cameron Raynes

Wakefield Press

Wakefield Press
16 Rose Street
Mile End
South Australia 5031
wakefieldpress.com.au

First published 2009
Reprinted 2018

Typeset by Wakefield Press

National Library of Australia Cataloguing-in-Publication entry

Author:	Raynes, Cameron, 1964– .
Title:	The last protector: the illegal removal of Aboriginal children from their parents in South Australia/Cameron Raynes.
ISBN:	978 1 862548 04 6 (pbk.).
Notes:	Includes index. Bibliography.
Subjects:	Children, Aboriginal Australian – South Australia – Removal. Aboriginal Australians – South Australia – Removal. Aboriginal Australians – South Australia – Treatment. Aboriginal Australians – South Australia – Child welfare. Children, Aboriginal Australian – South Australia. Children, Aboriginal Australian – Government policy – South Australia. Aboriginal Australians, Treatment of – South Australia – History. Children, Aboriginal Australian – Institutional care – South Australia. Child welfare – South Australia – History.
Dewey Number:	362.849915

Wakefield Press thanks
Coriole Vineyards for
their continued support

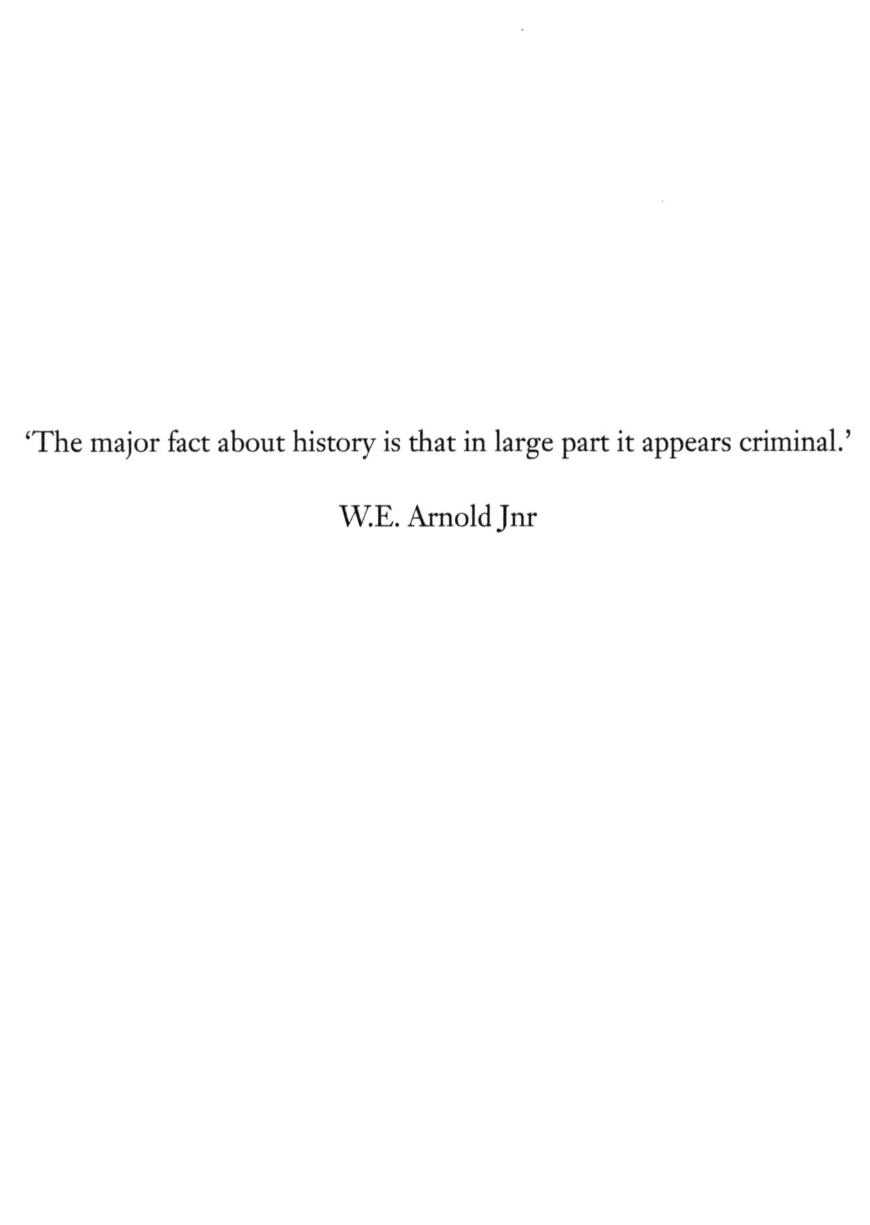

'The major fact about history is that in large part it appears criminal.'

W.E. Arnold Jnr

The actual names of all the Aboriginal people referred to in this work have been replaced by pseudonyms, including those which occur within extracts of correspondence. This has been done in order to protect their privacy, as many of them were the subject of very intrusive and personal forms of government scrutiny. The names of the white protagonists have not been altered.

CONTENTS

ABBREVIATIONS

AAM	Australian Aborigines Mission
ACA	Advisory Council of Aborigines
AFA	Aborigines' Friends' Association
APB	Aborigines Protection Board
CWD	Children's Welfare Department
CWPRB	Children's Welfare and Public Relief Board
CWPRD	Children's Welfare and Public Relief Department
GRG	Government Record Group
SCC	State Children's Council
SCD	State Children's Department
UAM	United Aborigines Mission

FOREWORD BY JULIAN BURNSIDE, QC

On 13 February 2008, in the first sitting of the new parliament, the newly elected Rudd Labor Government said 'sorry' to the Stolen Generations. It was an apology many had waited a long time to hear. And it was astonishing and uplifting to hear some of the noblest and most dignified sentiments ever uttered in that place on the hill. It is worth recalling some of the words:

> Today we honour the Indigenous peoples of this land, the oldest continuing cultures in human history. We reflect on their past mistreatment. We reflect in particular on the mistreatment of those who were Stolen Generations – this blemished chapter in our nation's history …
>
> We apologise for the laws and policies of successive Parliaments and Governments that have inflicted profound grief, suffering and loss on these our fellow Australians …
>
> For the pain, suffering and hurt of these stolen generations, their descendants and for their families left behind, we say sorry.
>
> To the mothers and the fathers, the brothers and the sisters, for the breaking up of families and communities, we say sorry.
>
> And for the indignity and degradation thus inflicted on a proud people and a proud culture, we say sorry …

This date will be remembered as a day the nation shifted, perceptibly. The apology marked a significant step in the process of reconciling ourselves with our past. It must have resonated especially in South Australia, a state which is still wrestling with its attitude to a disfigured history of relations with the Aboriginal people.

South Australia's legislation concerning Aboriginal people was subtly but importantly different from that in other states and territories. Unlike some jurisdictions, it did not vest uncontrolled powers in the hands of the protectors. The legislature had flirted with the idea of doing so. In October 1923, there was a proposal to allow the chief protector to remove illegitimate Aboriginal children at any age. The following exchange shows how coming events cast their shadows before:

Mr Gunn:	Who is to exercise the power of discretion?
Mr Hague:	The Chief Protector of Aborigines.
Mr Gunn:	If he has only to satisfy himself that there is neglect it is certainly an extensive power to place in the hands of one man.
Mr Hague:	He will not be very anxious to take away any child.
Mr Gunn:	We know what happens when we give power like this.

With the benefit of history, we do indeed know what happens when we give power like this, even when the power comes not from law but from circumstances. Because in South Australia the power to remove was ultimately quite narrowly circumscribed. The Aborigines Protection Board (APB) had to gain the agreement of the Children's Welfare and Public Relief Board (CWPRB) in order to take an Aboriginal child into care. The alternative was a court order, on proof that the child was neglected. Given that the APB was, by law, the guardian of Aboriginal children, a court order would be an embarrassment.

The CWPRB was not willing to lend itself to a program of removals driven by a policy of assimilation rather than by welfare concerns. The APB did not want the ignominy of court orders which, of necessity, would be predicated on the board's own failure to discharge its obligations as guardian. William Richard Penhall was last Chief Protector of Aborigines in South Australia, and was secretary of the APB from 1940 until 1953. He drove a system under which the APB, lacking legal power to remove Aboriginal children, simply removed children as the opportunity arose.

Penhall was, it seems, willing to give effect to the government's wishes regardless of the law; he was willing to treat Aboriginal people with astonishing harshness, despite the ostensibly beneficial purposes of the legislation he administered. He was an early example of that brand of public servant who conceives it his duty to implement government policy, rather than to administer the laws made by the parliament. And he added a dash of his own hard, punitive personality to the mix. He was prepared to deny food to Aboriginal parents if they did not agree to give up their children; he authorised the removal of children in full knowledge that to do so was beyond the APB's legal power; he facilitated the illegal detention of Aboriginal children in mission stations run by church bodies and helped conceal the illegality from the children and their parents alike. He was aware of, and complicit in, a system of forced child labour at the Koonibba Mission.

It is inconceivable that Penhall could have conducted the affairs of the APB for so long in this manner if he did not have the tacit support of the government and a majority of the population. But the legislation did not authorise what was done. Penhall had stamped the APB with his style. Four years after he retired, the APB was still removing Aboriginal children in the way it had for so long under his stewardship. One of the children, a boy removed in 1957 at the age of 13 months, sued the government 40 years later. He won. He was the only member of the Stolen Generations to have succeeded in a claim arising out of his removal.

Thus it was that South Australia had Aboriginal legislation which was, relatively speaking, enlightened, but a policy which was as bad as any other jurisdiction. It has the rare distinction to be the first Australian government to be found liable for the consequences of its policy of removal of Aboriginal children. It is probably not pitching it too high to say that South Australia has Penhall to thank for that uncomfortable distinction. In 1911 the APB reported to Parliament that

> The half-castes and quadroons are steadily replacing the blacks, who are slowly but surely dying out, and if they are left in the camps it will not be long before we shall have a race of nearly white people living like the Aborigines.

That possibility was plainly conceived to be unacceptable. Over the next 50 years the white man sought to erase the embarrassing traces of the original inhabitants of this land, ostensibly for their betterment.

Penhall's leadership of the APB brings to mind the observation of the Israeli philosopher Avishai Margalit who speaks of the

> ... fear that justice may lack compassion and might even be an expression of vindictiveness. There is a suspicion that the Just Society might become mired in rigid calculations of what is just, which may replace gentleness and humane consideration in simple human relations.

This book is the history of a dedicated but deeply flawed public servant; a man who put personal beliefs above humanity, and policy above law. It may be that the story told in this book only ended on 13 February 2008, although it may yet be too early to know.

PREFACE

The files we are not allowed to see

In November 2001, I was given permission by the Department of Aboriginal Affairs and Reconciliation (DAAR) to view the correspondence files of the Aborigines Department, dating back to 1866.

Over the next few years I spent many long days in the public reading room of State Records of South Australia, reverently opening up box after box of dusty, fragile letters and reports, unpacking and reading them from cover to cover. In all, I went through about 70 boxes, reading some 70,000 items of correspondence. I filled several exercise books with my notes.

As I read I noticed patterns. Most interestingly, there were discrepancies between the legal instruments available to the Aborigines Department and the practices of this department, especially in relation to the guardianship of Aboriginal children. A cryptic letter from the Crown Solicitor; a letter from Penhall to a concerned citizen in which he denied his department was doing anything wrong; a comment here; an unsigned note there. Slowly I became aware that there was a very important story scattered throughout these documents, waiting for someone to piece it together.

By 2003, I had the makings of a history. It would centre on the administration of the department under William Richard Penhall, the last Chief Protector of Aborigines in South Australia and the head of the department from 1939 to 1953. The central topic of this work would be the illegal removal of Aboriginal children from their parents.

It soon became clear that several pieces of the historical jigsaw were missing. There was no 'smoking gun', no unequivocal admission by Penhall or the Crown Solicitor that the department had overstepped its authority. However, I had heard of the existence of certain files in the possession of the Crown Solicitor's Office (CSO). I suspected that the information in these files went to the heart of the question as to whether the department had acted illegally in the 1940s and 1950s.

On the advice of State Records, I rang the CSO. I was told that the files in question may contain the legal opinion of the Crown Solicitor and so would not be made available to me. The CSO was mindful of the Bruce Trevorrow case, the landmark South Australian case for compensation by a member of the Stolen Generation. Clearly, they did not want anyone to access material that could shed light on the question of whether Trevorrow deserved compensation. It did not matter that the legal opinion dated back to the 1940s. The CSO suggested I write to the Attorney-General, the Hon. Michael Atkinson.

In December 2003 I did this. I was duly informed that the matter I raised was the responsibility of the Minister for Aboriginal Affairs. I pointed out to the Attorney-General that the files, though the property of DAAR, were in the possession of the Crown Solicitor, and it was he, not DAAR, who was denying me access to them. On 2 February 2004, I was finally informed by the Attorney-General that the matter I had raised was 'receiving attention'.

Finally, on 4 April, the Hon. Michael Atkinson wrote that the files in question attracted 'legal professional privilege' and therefore I would not be able to view them. His letter ended: 'I have written to DAAR and asked it to withdraw your authorisation to access files from GRG 52/1 until that series of documents has been checked.'

I was astounded. Not only was I being denied a viewing of these potentially explosive 'secret' files, my access to the *whole* of the correspondence of the Aborigines Department, all 170 boxes of it, was being revoked.

Two months later I again wrote to DAAR, requesting access to a single file from another government record group, GRG 52/10. File 8 of 1927 of that series contained, I understood, an application Penhall made in 1927 for the position of Superintendent of Point McLeay Station. It was a simple request for a simple file. Four years later, I am still waiting for a ruling.

I also requested of the Crown Solicitor's Office access to three other files from GRG 52/1. File 64 of 1949 contained correspondence between Penhall and the Assemblies of God Church; file 88a of 1950 concerned Aboriginal deaths at Ernabella Mission; and file 3 of 1953 included a flier for a meeting of the Aborigines Advancement League in Adelaide. I was reasonably confident that none of these files contained any advice from the Crown Solicitor – nothing that could be subject to legal professional privilege. A week after I made this request, the CSO officer concerned informed me that she had forgotten my request! She assured me that she would get onto it as soon as possible.

Two weeks later I rang again. The officer advised me that she had done nothing because my permission to view GRG 52/1 had been withdrawn. It was official. Michael Atkinson had delivered on his promise and had me effectively banned from accessing GRG 52/1.

An officer at DAAR then told me that every time I wanted to look at *anything* from GRG 52/1 it would have to be retrieved from State Records – staff resources permitting – and examined for the presence of material subject to legal professional privilege. If the file I requested contained no such material, a request for its release would be submitted to the CEO of DAAR, who would then submit a request to the Attorney-General. I requested a clear outline of this new access regime, in writing. I am still waiting.

This new regime was then extended to all members of the South Australian public. It is still in place as I write this, in June 2008.

*

This book exposes deficiencies of the Aborigines Department in South Australia under William Penhall's term as its administrative head, from 1939 to 1953. It examines the circumstances and manner in which his department removed or withheld Aboriginal children from their parents. The evidence drawn from the state government's own archives strongly suggests that they were at times taken *illegally*. Such a claim has not yet been sustained for any government in Australia – federal, state or territory.

In the course of presenting this case, the book shows how Penhall exerted autocratic control over Aboriginal people through bluff and threat. It uncovers his department's carefully cultivated secrecy, which prevented most South Australians knowing of the oppressive regime under which Aboriginal people lived. It makes tangible to the reader the culture of negativity which festered under Penhall, and the moral and legal irresponsibility of his staff. Their deliberate and sustained attempts to mislead the Aboriginal people of South Australia will be documented throughout this book.

Is it possible that the people specifically charged with the protection and development of Aboriginal people could have been part of such a program? Consider the words of A.P. Elkin, one of the founders of Australian anthropology. In the last essay he wrote, 50 years on from the events in question, Elkin finally felt able to speak of his fieldwork experiences of the late 1920s in north-western Australia:

> The generally accepted principle was that Aborigines had to be kept in their place. Even a government officer, a Protector of Aborigines, who had contributed to the costs arising from a punitive expedition in 1926, explained that Aborigines had to be given a lesson from time to time. Apparently it was only incidental that this particular lesson involved killing and burning the bodies of 20 or more Aborigines in 'revenge' for the fatal spearing of one European …
>
> It was only a minor incident when this same Protector kicked and cursed a young Aboriginal stockman for asking for a shirt and a pair of trousers to replace those he had passed to his 'uncle' …[1]

We will see this 'generally accepted principle' played out relentlessly in the mid twentieth century among the ranks of the government and the public service in South Australia. In 1911, which is where this book begins, the culture of kicking and cursing was already well established.

*

CHAPTER ONE

'The blacks' camp', 1911–1920

'THE HALF-CASTES AND QUADROONS ARE STEADILY REPLACING THE BLACKS, WHO ARE SLOWLY BUT SURELY DYING OUT, AND IF THEY ARE LEFT IN THE CAMPS IT WILL NOT BE LONG BEFORE WE SHALL HAVE A RACE OF NEARLY WHITE PEOPLE LIVING LIKE THE ABORIGINES.'

SOUTH AUSTRALIA, PARLIAMENT 1911, ANNUAL REPORT OF ABORIGINES DEPARTMENT, 16 SEPTEMBER 1911, GRG 52/1/1911/29

On 3 July 1911, W.G. South, ex-policeman and Protector of Aborigines, was alerted to the fact that a nine-year-old 'quarter-caste' girl, Rose Latham, was at Nilpena Station.[1] South enlisted police officers to remove Rose from the station while her mother was away. She was brought before a court, charged with being a neglected child and sent to Edwardstown Industrial School, to remain there until she turned 18.[2] South visited Rose a month later and argued:

> She is almost white and has scarcely a trace of Aboriginal features. To have left her to the inevitable fate of all half-caste girls brought up in the blacks camp in the interior would have been, to say the least of it, cruel.
>
> The half-castes and quadroons are steadily replacing the blacks, who are slowly but surely dying out, and if they are left in the camps it will not be long before we shall have a race of nearly white people living like the Aborigines.[3]

Just days before this report was submitted, the manager of Nilpena Station wrote to the Port Augusta police, requesting the return of Rose:

> The mother (who is also a half caste) was away at Hergott at the time and didn't

> know anything about it until she returned to Stuarts Creek a few days later. She is now in a terrible state of mind over the loss of her child, and she came to me in a most pitiable manner to ask me to get her child back.
>
> This affair has caused great consternation amongst the blacks in the camp here, and on that account, & the sorrowing mother, I ask you respectfully to use your influence in getting the child returned to its mother.[4]

South refused this request, advising the manager that Rose's mother could 'rest assured that the child is in good hands and well cared for'.[5]

At the time, there were over 800 'half-castes and quadroons' and 4000 'full-blooded' Aboriginal people in South Australia.[6] Both groups were apparently 'on the rise', and this had translated into pressure on the state government to enact legislation to deal more effectively with them. The *Aborigines Act 1911* was introduced, and the Aborigines Department (the department) created and placed under the control of the Commissioner of Public Works.

Under the Act, the chief protector was now the legal guardian of 'every aboriginal and half-caste child'.[7] In addition, the Act allowed the chief protector to keep 'any aboriginal or half-caste' within the boundaries of any reserve or Aboriginal institution.[8] This included any mission station, orphanage or home used 'for the benefit, care, or protection of the aboriginal inhabitants of the State'. The premier, John Verran, agreed that this clause allowed Aboriginal children to be removed from their parents and sent to an institution.[9] This interpretation was to be questioned in the late 1940s, as we will see.

In fact, the removal of Aboriginal children had been happening in a surreptitious manner for several years. In November 1909, South had asked the Commissioner of Police to help with the general committal of 'half-caste' children to the State Children's Department (SCD).[10] This followed his receipt, seven days earlier, of an extraordinary police document which listed all known 'half-castes' in South Australia. This document named 766 'half-castes', with indications of their age, locality, and whether they were living in a house or camp.[11]

Four Aboriginal children from Oodnadatta were committed to the SCD on 5 February 1910.[12] By mid-1911, the State Children's Council (SCC) had decided they would take charge of 'half-caste' children between one and seven years of age, in such numbers and at such times as was 'politic'.[13] Their report for 1910/1911 concluded:

> The best mode of dealing with aboriginal half-caste, quadroon, and octoroon

> children has occupied a considerable portion of the Council's time and thought during the year ... It was finally decided, after consultation with the Protector of Aborigines, to administer the law as it stands, by as far as possible gathering into the Council's care all neglected illegitimate aboriginal half-caste, quadroon, and octoroon children, and paying special attention to the girls, as needing the earliest and most complete protection.

The removal of Aboriginal children continued throughout the first few years of the operation of the Act. In May 1913, South visited Bordertown at the request of the Commissioner of Public Works to investigate the circumstances of several 'light-skinned' Aboriginal children. He wrote to the commissioner:

> I have the honor to inform you that I visited the Native camps at Bordertown on the 10th instant, but owing to the short time I could remain there, I was not able to get full particulars of the names, ages and circumstances of two families of half-caste and quadroon children living in the camps, but what I saw leads me to think the children should be at once removed and placed under the State Children's Department. Two of the children are white, with blue eyes, and one has auburn hair.[14]

These children included the four children of Andrew Allan. In June 1913, Mounted Constable Redpath reported that although the children's mother had died, two of their aunts lived with the family, the eldest two children attended the state school and Andrew was in full-time employment:

> They live in two rooms, the interior of same having a clean appearance. The children are white and were neatly dressed, and evidently fairly well looked after.[15]

Nevertheless, on 1 July 1913, the secretary of the SCC requested that the Bordertown police charge the children as being 'neglected [and under] unfit guardianship'.[16] Within three weeks, all four of Allan's children had been sent to the Industrial School at Magill, with three children from another family similarly dealt with.[17] In their annual report for 1913/1914, the SCC argued that the 'problem' of 'half-caste children' would be greatly relieved if those members of the general population who required 'coachmen, grooms, and other domestic servants would take aboriginal, half-caste children, and adolescents'.[18]

By mid 1915, there were 54 Aboriginal children under the control of the SCC, with 48 of them placed with white families in country and suburban locations, two in the Industrial School, three in the Girls' Probationary School, and one in the Lying-in Home at Magill.[19]

On 10 May 1917, the first Regulations were made under the Aborigines Act to allow the chief protector to expel any Aboriginal person from any or every institution if he was of the opinion that, among other things, the person in question was 'habitually disorderly, lazy, disobedient, insolent, intemperate, or immoral'; that their presence was 'inimical to the maintenance of discipline or good order in an aboriginal institution'; or that they had been found guilty of two or more of a list of 12 offences. These included intoxication; 'immoral or disgraceful conduct'; the use of 'profane, blasphemous, obscene, abusive, or insulting language'; insubordination; being an able-bodied person over the age of 14 years who did not attempt to find employment outside the institution; being 'dirty or untidy'; or failing to keep dwellings clean and in good order.[20]

Nineteen months later, five new offences were added to the list.[21] Among other things it was now an offence to play 'any game in any street or road' within an Aboriginal institution without first obtaining the permission of its superintendent. It was an oppressive and hostile regime that confronted the Aboriginal inhabitants of South Australia.

CHAPTER TWO

'In the hands of one man', 1921–1938

> ALLEN: THE GREATEST CARE SHOULD BE TAKEN IN A MATTER OF THIS KIND, AND THIS AMENDMENT IS NOT LIKELY TO MAKE MATTERS MUCH BETTER FROM THE NATIVE MOTHER'S POINT OF VIEW ...
> GUNN: WHO IS TO EXERCISE THE POWER OF DISCRETION?
> HAGUE: THE CHIEF PROTECTOR OF ABORIGINES.
> GUNN: IF HE HAS ONLY TO SATISFY HIMSELF THAT THERE IS NEGLECT IT IS CERTAINLY AN EXTENSIVE POWER TO PLACE IN THE HANDS OF ONE MAN.
> HAGUE: HE WILL NOT BE VERY ANXIOUS TO TAKE AWAY ANY CHILD.
> GUNN: WE KNOW WHAT HAPPENS WHEN WE GIVE POWER LIKE THIS.
>
> **SOUTH AUSTRALIA, HOUSE OF ASSEMBLY 1923, DEBATES, VOL. 1, P. 738**

By 1921, there were 90 'half-caste' children under the age of 14 at Point Pearce Station on Yorke Peninsula, with another 81 at Point McLeay Station on the shores of Lake Alexandrina. William Hague, the Commissioner of Public Works, argued that these children regarded these government stations as 'a permanent home from which they cannot be turned away', and that it was time to make 'determined efforts to apprentice them out':

> They must be taken away from their present environment at the stations, from contact with the older 'half-castes' and their evil associations, and set to work in a new atmosphere ... and they must be taken in hand young.[1]

How to do this though? The Act only allowed for indefinite detention at 'Aboriginal institutions', themselves the source of these 'evil associations'. Aboriginal children could be dealt with under the *State Children Act 1895*, but under this Act, a child considered at risk was to be brought before a justice of the peace, who could declare the child 'neglected' after considering the evidence before him. This was considered 'needlessly cumbersome and unnecessarily public'.

New legislation was drafted. The Aborigines (Half Caste Children) Bill allowed for the simple, quick removal of an Aboriginal child from his or her parents. An Aboriginal child could be transferred from the control of the chief protector to the State Children's Council (SCC), simply upon the signing of a form. This would then allow the child to be treated as a ward of state, and so placed in a detention centre, training centre or with an employer.

In parliament, Henry Tossell, the Liberal member for Yorke Peninsula, called the Bill 'one of the cruellest things I have ever heard of'.[2] Even Malcolm McIntosh, the Liberal member for Albert, who was to have ministerial responsibility for the Aborigines Department (the department) throughout Penhall's reign, opposed the notion of taking 'half-caste' children away from their parents.[3] The Bill lapsed.

However, this 'transfer of control' mechanism was preserved in the Bill brought before parliament in 1923 – the Aborigines (Training of Children) Bill. It would allow the chief protector, with the approval of the SCC, to commit certain Aboriginal children to any state children's institution until the age of 18, there to be treated 'as if such child were a neglected child'.[4] It was to apply to all illegitimate Aboriginal children who were neglected in the opinion of the chief protector and the SCC. It was to apply also to legitimate Aboriginal children who had either obtained their qualifying certificate or who were 14 or older, regardless of whether they were considered neglected. This was aimed squarely at the inhabitants of the government stations.

In the Legislative Council, Thomas McCallum, pastoralist and member of the Liberal Party, spoke against the Bill, advocating the placing of Aboriginal people 'among the farmers and on stations' where they could find work:

> I have great respect for family life and that should not be broken up ... Those people have the same love for their children as have the best of the white population.[5]

In early October 1923, the treasurer, William Hague, the member for Barossa, proposed an alteration to the Bill to allow the chief protector to remove an illegitimate child at any age, rather than only at nine months or older as had been suggested. The following, prophetic exchange took place:

> Allen: The greatest care should be taken in a matter of this kind, and this amendment is not likely to make matters much better from the native mother's point of view ... I hope the Minister will have the clause so

	safeguarded that only in extreme cases will it be put into operation.
Gunn:	Who is to exercise the power of discretion?
Hague:	The Chief Protector of Aborigines.
Gunn:	If he has only to satisfy himself that there is neglect it is certainly an extensive power to place in the hands of one man.
Hague:	He will not be very anxious to take away any child.
Gunn:	We know what happens when we give power like this.[6]

The *Aborigines (Training of Children) Act 1923* was assented to on 14 November 1923. In its final form it *did* allow the chief protector to transfer his control of illegitimate Aboriginal children to the SCC *regardless of their age*.

The new chief protector, Francis Garnett, moved quickly to use the new Act. In January 1924, he requested of the superintendents of Point Pearce, Point McLeay, and of the missioner-in-charge of the Lutherans' Koonibba Mission near Ceduna, the names of all children between the ages of 13 and 15 for 'training on intended lines'.[7] These children were to be transferred to the SCC and removed to a training centre or sent out to work. In March 1924, he sent the secretary of the SCC a list of recommended children. The necessary paperwork was prepared. Twenty-two children from Point McLeay and 16 from Point Pearce were targeted.[8]

However, before the plan could be implemented, there was a public relations disaster for the department. The first actual transfer of control was that of a young boy, who, in early March 1924, was forcibly removed from his mother at the Adelaide train station by police, in full view of the public.[9]

An outcry erupted, with Reverends Taplin and Sexton, the latter a member of the Advisory Council of Aborigines (ACA), among a number of commentators subjecting the department to public scrutiny and criticism. Two months after apprehending the boy, the SCC was forced to return him to his mother.

On the same day he received a letter from Sexton criticising the removal of the boy at the train station, Garnett advised his commissioner that 'after careful consideration' he had come to the conclusion that the administration of the 1923 Act should be suspended, 'and that other methods should be employed in dealing with the question, especially avoiding the breaking up of families'.[10] The Act became a virtual 'dead letter'.

Given this publicity disaster, it is ironic that this Act was established precisely in order to conceal the removal of Aboriginal children. The 'transfer of control' mechanism was clearly designed to take deliberations about Aboriginal custody out of the court system, and so, out of the public arena.

This may have been thought necessary for various reasons. In particular, it may have been apparent to some in the government that, the chief protector being the legal guardian of all Aboriginal children, he could hardly bring a successful court case against an Aboriginal parent for the neglect of their child. The responsibility for the welfare of all Aboriginal children, after all, belonged to the chief protector himself.[11]

The ACA had been established in 1918, to report and make recommendations on 'any matter connected with the protection, control, training, or education of, or otherwise affecting the interests of, the aboriginal and half-caste inhabitants of the State'.[12] By 1925, it had established its presence. When Chief Protector Garnett advised his commissioner of extensions required to the hospital at Point Pearce Station, he was very mindful of the ACA's opinion on the matter. Indeed, it appears he required their approval for the proposal to proceed.[13]

In 1925 the Regulations were changed to include the chief protector on the ACA, presumably to curb its influence.[14] Years later, Milroy Trail McLean, Garnett's successor as chief protector, wrote:

> I was never in agreement with the idea of the Chief Protector being a Member of the Committee, because I considered it defeated the object for which the Committee was appointed and often placed the Protector in an awkward position.
>
> If the Council is to bring the citizens viewpoint before the Government the Protector should not be involved in their resolutions ...[15]

When the ACA was formed there had been promises of a 'new order' in Aboriginal affairs. With a growing recognition among the Aboriginal population that this had failed to materialise, unrest resulted. In August 1926, two members of parliament visited Point Pearce to listen to the concerns of its Aboriginal residents. The meeting resulted in the compilation of a list of questions including 'Why are Whites allowed to share farm the Station land?' and 'Why are the houses for which we are paying rent not looked after?'[16]

The climate was no warmer at Point McLeay Station where, in October 1926, a prominent Aboriginal leader was fined for a breach of the Regulation which made it an offence for an Aboriginal person over the age of 14 to not seek employment outside the station. At the time, many Aboriginal people residing at the station found it difficult to secure outside employment.

At a meeting in the station church a petition was signed by 51 Aboriginal residents. They demanded that the ACA be made into a board of protection and that an Aboriginal person be appointed as a sub-protector.

William Harvey (MP) and Reverend John Sexton, the chairman and secretary respectively of the ACA, conducted an investigation and made a list of recommendations, mainly regarding discipline and punishment on the station. They requested a relaxation of the 'hostile' regime in place.[17] At this point, latent tension between the department and the ACA surfaced, with Ramsey, the superintendent of Point McLeay, making the bizarre accusation that the ACA had sent the Aboriginal leader there as a spy, in order to compile a list of grievances.[18] Within 10 months Ramsey had resigned, with William Richard Penhall taking over as superintendent in August 1927. He was to enjoy a relatively uncontroversial time at Point McLeay for the next two years.

The Children's Welfare and Public Relief Board (CWPRB) succeeded the SCC in April 1927, and, unlike its predecessor, was 'increasingly willing to attempt ... family maintenance' as an alternative to the removal of children.[19]

However, the existence of 'half-castes' in rural areas continued to work on the minds of South Australia's parliamentarians. On 1 December 1927, Thomas Butterfield, the Labor member for Newcastle, called for strict segregation of black and white and hoped for a South Australian future without the former: 'I say that from the white man's point of view, when the last black woman dies it will be a benefit to the people of this State.'[20] The tension between the ACA and the department remained. Chairman Harvey requested of the commissioner that he supply the ACA with budget estimates for the coming year.[21] Garnett promptly recommended that the request not be granted given 'the necessity for economy in expenditure'.[22] The commissioner's reply to Garnett reads, in full: 'Information not to be furnished.'[23]

Four months later, Garnett retired from his position as chief protector, and was succeeded by Milroy Trail McLean, the department's accountant.[24] Two months later, Garnett was appointed to the ACA.[25] The commissioner now had two of his men – the chief protector and the former chief protector – on this supposedly independent body.

Penhall's physical and emotional condition appears to have deteriorated during 1930, to the extent that in November of that year he was diagnosed as suffering from 'nervous exhaustion' and was unable to work for three weeks.[26] He returned to Point McLeay, only to leave again on 23 December, telling McLean 'that he could not carry on at the station'.[27] He was given another three weeks' leave.

In early January 1931, McLean offered him a lifeline. He could commence duties in the Adelaide office at his present salary as the department's accountant and clerk.[28] At the time, the effects of the Depression in South Australia were 'as severe as elsewhere in Australia, and in some ways worse'.[29] Penhall would have been very aware of the hardships affecting the thousands of unemployed in Adelaide and he readily accepted McLean's offer.[30]

McLean found it increasingly difficult to work with the ACA at their monthly meetings and, in March 1933, the regulation which declared that the chief protector would be a member of the ACA was revoked.[31] Years later, John McInnes, railway worker and Labor Commissioner of Public Works, made it clear that, in his mind, the Aboriginal 'problem' had arisen largely because of the attitudes of the female members of the ACA, who 'have always clamoured for special treatment for aborigines'. It was clear he had no time for the 'unpractical women' who sat on the council:

> During my term of office I took action which resulted in the Aborigines Advisory Council ceasing to exist for a considerable period. I did not consider that it was of any value and a good deal of my opinion was formed for me by people who had practical experience on the subject.[32]

In July 1933, McLean brought to the attention of the CWPRD the case of Sylvia Reid, the pregnant mother of three illegitimate children at Point Pearce. In one of the first such requests for several years, he asked that her children be taken from her:

> Superintendent Bray states that [Sylvia] is lazy and dirty and neglects her children and he recommends that the children be committed to the care of your Department and the mother placed in a home where she would have to work for her keep and confinement expenses.[33]

The CWPRD moved quickly to investigate the matter, visiting Sylvia at the station. Two weeks later, the chairman of the CWPRB wrote:

> The Superintendent of the Mission, and the Chief Protector of Aboriginals are both of the opinion that the girl should be placed in a home where she would have to work before and after her confinement, and that her children should be committed to the care of this Department. I would respectfully point out that this department knows of no law which would permit of a woman being compulsorily

> placed in any Refuge or Institution ...
>
> So far as the children are concerned, if they are 'neglected' children, then they can be dealt with in the usual way ... Whether it is necessary to commit these children because they are in an unfit home is a matter to be decided by the Court ...[34]

Indeed, three years before this, the chairman had noted that, in relation to another Aboriginal child, there was a clear process to follow:

> The only other way in which the child can be dealt with by this Department would be if he were committed as a 'neglected' or 'destitute' child by a Court. Notice of such complaint would have to be given to the parent, and the opportunity given him to place the child in some fit home before a mandate is likely to be granted.[35]

It appears that nothing further happened in regard to the Sylvia Reid case. Over the next 20 years, as we shall see, the CWPRB held to its opinion that Aboriginal parents should enjoy the same legal rights and be subjected to the same legal processes that applied to white parents.

Later the next year, McLean was absent for eight weeks, suffering from 'nervous debility'.[36] He took a sea voyage to Colombo to recuperate[37], and Penhall was made acting chief protector.[38]

On 18 October 1934, John Lyons, wheat farmer, grazier and Liberal Country League member for Stanley, led a parliamentary debate on the Aboriginal-less future that Butterfield had advocated seven years earlier. The following exchange took place:

> Lyons: In his consideration of the welfare of the aborigines has the Minister considered the suggestion of the biological experiment of breeding the aboriginals white, which might be accomplished in a few generations, and which would rid us of this eternal problem?
>
> Hudd: Not yet.[39]

The attitude of successive state governments to the department can be summed up in an exchange which took place in parliament in 1936, between Baden Pattinson and McInnes, ex-Commissioner of Public Works:

Pattinson: Furthermore it cannot be said that the care of our aborigines has been the main concern of the State. It has been carried on by a relatively small branch of the Public Works Department. Why it was ever attached to that department no one has ever been able to explain to me satisfactorily and I am quite sure that the present Commissioner of Public Works and some of his equally estimable predecessors have often wondered why they have been saddled with this somewhat distasteful task.

McInnes: No one else wanted it.[40]

Pattinson picked up on the growing concern among Aboriginal people, interested observers, and some of his colleagues that the department had for too long been left to drift without aims or policies. In parliament, he presented a petition from 161 Aboriginal residents of South Australia, pleading:

> that the House take steps to provide for their better treatment, the better education of their children, and proper opportunities for their advancement; and asking that the House take steps to appoint an Aboriginal Protection Board, on which the aboriginal inhabitants and their descendants should have direct representation in order to provide for their advancement.[41]

Finally, a Bill was introduced to allow for the ACA to be replaced by a board. Under the Bill, however, the chief protector would become the chairman of the board. This did not sit well with several parties. Daniel Davies, the Member for Yorke Peninsula, argued that it was an insult to the Aborigines' Friends' Association (AFA) that the Bill had been drafted in consultation with the chief protector and the Public Service Commissioner only.[42] He noted:

> As emphasised by my colleague [i.e. Pattinson], very particular care has been taken in this Bill to preserve the position of certain men. The welfare and improvement of the aborigines and half-castes were apparently regarded as being of far less importance.[43]

When an amendment to the Bill that would make the chief protector the *secretary* of the board was passed by the Legislative Council, the Bill was promptly dropped.[44]

The notion of 'breeding the aboriginals white' was taken up again in parliament in November 1936.[45] Indeed, it can be argued that the 'biological experiment' was already well under way in an unofficial sense. For years, those children categorised as being 'half-caste', or of lesser amount of Aboriginal blood, and living in remote parts of the state, had been targeted by authorities. The fairer the child, the more at risk they were of being removed from their family, especially Aboriginal girls. Throughout the 1930s, police in remote areas, at the request of missionary organisations, removed Aboriginal children from their parents and sent them to the United Aborigines Mission's Colebrook Home, at Quorn in the southern Flinders Ranges.

In August 1937, Protector George Aiston, an ex-policeman, noted that young Aboriginal men were leaving the Marree district to find wives, an exodus he put down to the loss of female 'half-caste' babies which had begun more than 20 years before under the policies of removal.[46] In this regard, consider the SCC's stated aims in their program of Aboriginal child removal as outlined in their report of 1910/1911:

> The Council is fully persuaded of the importance of prompt action *in order to prevent the growth of a race* that would rapidly increase in numbers, attain a maturity without education or religion, and become a menace to the morals and health of the community [emphasis added].[47]

Apparently, the SCC believed its role was to limit the ability of a racially defined group to reproduce itself. It can be argued that this is evidence of a program of genocide.[48] The SCC's program appears to have been relatively successful in some parts of the state.

In September 1938, McLean had another breakdown. By the end of the month he had been on sick leave for four weeks and had applied for another month off.[49] Penhall – lifelong Methodist and occasional lay preacher – was again made acting chief protector.[50] In a spectacular fall from grace, McLean accepted the position of clerk in the Vermin Branch of the Lands Department.[51]

Another Bill to amend the Aborigines Act was presented to the South Australian Parliament in 1938. Penhall maintained that the head of the department should be the chairman, and not the secretary, of the new board.[52] This was the formula that had been defeated in 1936. In any case, Penhall was confident that the status quo would prevail even if he was *not* chairman:

> Whilst the appointment of a chairman other than the departmental head may

> create some little difficulty ... I think the head of the department possessing a complete knowledge of the activities of the department could and would in actual practice exert a controlling influence on the Members of the Board and to a great extent frame the policy of the Board. For instance, he would prepare the business, submit recommendations and introduce the various matters to be considered at meetings of the Board.[53]

In this he was to prove very perceptive. Departmental and government disinterest in the ACA was to be mirrored in their dealings with the Aborigines Protection Board over the next decade and more, rendering that body virtually impotent.

CHAPTER THREE

'This practice has no regulation to support it', 1939–1946

'THE DIFFICULTY ABOUT THE BABY IS THAT I CANNOT PROVE THAT [ALLY] HAS NEGLECTED THE CHILD, OR THAT SHE IS NOT CAPABLE OF CARING FOR HIM. I WILL WATCH THE SITUATION CAREFULLY, AND TRY TO GET [ALLY] TO AGREE TO PLACING HIM IN A HOME. THIS IS THE ONLY COURSE OPEN TO ME, AS I COULD NOT SUCCEED IN ANY ACTION THROUGH THE COURTS TO TAKE HIM AWAY FROM HIS MOTHER.'

PENHALL TO WRIGHT, WARRAKIMBA STATION, 2 MARCH 1943, GRG52/1/1943/12

On 25 April 1939, Thomas Playford, the new Premier of South Australia, Robert Richards, the Leader of the Opposition and A.J. Hannan, the Crown Solicitor, were among a group of 'representative citizens of Adelaide' who, in the face of the looming war, released a manifesto for 'moral rearmament' on Anzac Day. Unfortunately, this did not extend to revising policy in relation to Aboriginal affairs.

On 3 September 1939, Australia's citizen, naval, army and air forces were called out for war service. In debate on the new Aborigines Bill, Malcolm McIntosh, the minister responsible for the Aborigines Department throughout the period of Penhall's reign, made it clear that in his view the chief impediment to Aboriginal progress was the Aboriginal people themselves.[1] Over the next 14 years he would make little attempt to inform himself of Aboriginal issues and concerns, happy to concentrate on the more high-profile of his responsibilities, which included public works, railways and local government.

Government disinterest in Aboriginal affairs was not confined to the responsible minister. Playford, who would be the premier for the whole of Penhall's reign as secretary of the board, believed that the provision of social welfare benefits was inimical to economic growth.[2] Where he was interested in

Aboriginal affairs, it was mainly in terms of the possibility of cutting back on spending.[3]

For Playford, the social services, health, the arts, even education, were 'non-productive' aspects of government responsibility. His central goal was to ensure the state's full recovery from the Depression, and he would do this through generous incentives to primary producers and the development of secondary industry on a scale not seen before in South Australia. There was little or no pressure from within his government to alter this program. His Cabinet for most of this period 'consisted of men who represented rural constituencies ... [with] little more formal education than the Premier'[4], which was negligible.

'Aboriginal Sunday' was initiated on 28 January 1940, following a call by the South Australian Council of Churches. This religious day, recognising the presence and contribution of Aboriginal people, was observed throughout the Commonwealth. In Adelaide, Dr Charles Duguid, the founder of the Ernabella Mission, a tireless advocate for Aboriginal people and Penhall's personal physician, conducted the morning sermon at the Stow Church. In the evening, after the service at St Peter's Cathedral, he was reported to have said that the laws relating to Aboriginal people were 'appalling'.[5]

Four days later, the amended *Aborigines Act 1934–1939* came into operation, allowing the creation of the Aborigines Protection Board (the board).[6] The initial appointments to it included Professor J.B. Cleland and Dr Charles Duguid.[7] Penhall was made the secretary of the board.[8]

The new Act broadened the definition of 'Aborigine' to include 'all persons descended from the original inhabitants of Australia'. However, where the board was now of the opinion that an Aboriginal person was, 'by reason of his character and standard of intelligence and development', deserving of exemption from the Act, that person could be so exempted. Such persons would no longer be considered to be Aborigines.

Now it was the *board* that was the legal guardian of all Aboriginal children. The section of the Act allowing the detention of any Aboriginal person at an Aboriginal reserve or institution remained but, again, the authority to do this was vested in the board.

At the time, similar guardianship arrangements operated in Western Australia, Queensland and the Northern Territory. The consensus among present-day writers is that guardianship provisions in these jurisdictions allowed their protectors or boards to remove Aboriginal children from their parents and place them where they saw fit.[9] One writer has argued that such a guardian 'stands *in loco parentis* to the child and thus has parental responsibilities'.[10]

However, in 1951, Penhall was to write: 'The Aborigines Protection Board has no power or authority to remove children from their mothers, and in fact have never done so.'[11]

How do we explain this discrepancy, which suggests that any removals which occurred under Penhall were of an *illegal* nature?

As early as September 1941, Penhall was aware that some of the directions he gave had no legal standing. When Mrs Thomas, of Port Germein, requested that her daughter be released from the Umeewarra Mission Children's Home at Port Augusta, Penhall wrote: 'You have entered into an agreement with Mrs. Wyld to allow [Denise] to remain in the Home ... until she is 16 years of age, and the agreement must be carried out.'[12]

To Mrs Wyld, the wife of the missionary at Umeewarra, he confided:

> I doubt very much whether the agreement has any legal value. However, I will advise Mrs. [Thomas] that, as she has entered into an agreement to allow [Denise] to remain until she is 16 years of age, I cannot agree to her being released.[13]

In such ways, Penhall used his 'actual', as opposed to 'legal' authority, to remove or withhold Aboriginal children from their families.[14] There is other evidence that Penhall was prepared to ignore the law in dealing with Aboriginal people. In November 1939, he confided to Chinnery, the Director of Native Affairs in Darwin: 'At Point Pearce the Superintendent inflicts punishment on working natives guilty of minor offences, by fining them small sums. This practice has no regulation to support it.'[15]

In July 1940, five months into the board's new regime, Arthur Peel of the United Aborigines Mission (UAM) attacked its lack of direction: 'Do you intend to continue the present policy (or lack of policy) indefinitely in the vague hope that for no particular reason the natives will drift away and settle somewhere else?'[16]

Penhall responded to this by echoing his minister's claim that Aboriginal people were responsible for their own predicament, and arguing that efforts towards 'establishing the natives' had failed 'due primarily to the laziness of the natives, and secondarily to the lack of funds'.[17] He noted that '30 years experience amongst the natives has not begotten in me any undue optimism', and 'regretted' the 'tone' of Peel's letter.

Peel was not to be put off. He wrote again:

> I have often wondered whether the Department did have any really constructive policy in regard to the Aborigines. No doubt you have; but honestly, sir, since I have been at Swan Reach I have seen little evidence of it; and in the several interviews I have had with you you have never outlined it. I have just perused your Report for the year ended 30th June, 1939, and I can find little there to indicate that a policy calculated to permanently solve the Aboriginal problem is being pursued.[18]

Others in the UAM were only too happy with the board's lack of policy. It allowed them to push their own agenda of removing as many Aboriginal children from their parents as they could. In September 1942, A.B. Erskine, the secretary of the UAM, wrote:

> To sum up our attitude we will encourage and help the Native to help himself, and cause him to appreciate the Mission and make it worth his while co-operating. If a native is troublesome and negligent he will be warned, perhaps rent increased and as a last resort expelled from Reserve for a period, or life, *but his children retained* (with your Board's co-operation) [emphasis added].[19]

In any case, as far as the UAM were concerned, Aboriginal children were to be separated from their parents and placed into dormitories: 'We are definitely convinced that removal of the children from the mixed native environment is the only way to accomplish any real advance in their uplift ...'[20]

In pursuing this aim, the UAM often found itself in conflict with the parents of these children. Much of the conflict can be attributed to the UAM's steadfast refusal to offer respite care to Aboriginal parents, instead accepting Aboriginal children into their children's homes only if an agreement was entered into by the parents 'to leave the children there permanently'[21], or at least until they finished their schooling.

In parliament, two men formed an unlikely alliance in their attempts to bring Aboriginal issues to the notice of the government. Lindsay Riches, the Labor member for Stuart, was a lay preacher and the editor and proprietor of Port Augusta's weekly newspaper, *The Transcontinental*. Arthur Christian, the Liberal Country League member for Eyre, was a schoolteacher, wheat grower and grazier. Their efforts over several decades would be almost entirely wasted. They were up against a hardened attitude towards Aboriginal people, which was present throughout South Australian society, but distilled into pure indifference among the members of the ruling party, the Liberal Country League.

Not even the clergy were immune from the popular pastime of blaming the victim. In November 1940, Reverend Wood wrote to Penhall regarding the 'peculiar "lethargic" state of mind I have noticed as characteristic of the Aborigines'. He confided that the conditions at the Aboriginal camp at Iron Knob were 'deplorable' and bemoaned the fact that 'we as a nation have never really tried to educate them to appreciate a higher standard of living'. Despite this, he was opposed to the alleviation of their circumstances through the provision of better goods and services: 'I do not feel that better housing really would solve the problem, nor better clothes or food.'[22]

Penhall was quick to endorse his pessimism:

> The contents of your letter express my own convictions held for many years as a result of native contact over a long period. We may surround the aborigines with all kinds of regulations and prohibitions on the one hand, and inducements and encouragements on the other, but, until they themselves desire a higher standard of living, I fear very little can be done for them.[23]

It is unclear what Penhall meant by 'inducements and encouragements'. Aboriginal people at the time were denied such basic things as pensions, maternity allowances and the right to vote in federal elections. Very little of the public purse was spent for their betterment; very little was actually 'done for them'. The 'average cost per Aborigine' for the year ended 30 June 1940, was £4 12s 3d, which included capital expenditure on the government stations.[24] Many Aboriginal people throughout the state lived in conditions of gross poverty, and were dependent upon the supply of rations and blankets to get by.

Dr Duguid summed up the hypocrisy of the position that Wood and Penhall had reached when he raised the issue of Aboriginal discontent with their conditions at Swan Reach, where they lived in 'bag humpies' – huts lined with flour bags:

> The area assigned to these people ... is utterly inadequate in size, and very poor in quality – merely sand – and much of it is below flood level.
>
> One minute the native is described as being content with any lot, and having no ambition to rise. The next we refuse him a house. The reaction on the settlement is obvious. 'Hope deferred maketh the heart sick'.[25]

Penhall's inability to empathise with the Aboriginal people he was charged with assisting can be linked to his career within the department. As with McLean,

Penhall had been made chief protector from the position of departmental accountant. This tradition was probably designed to give the head of the department a grounding in the paucity of resources available to them. Further, since the first appointment in 1911, the chief protector had always been chosen from within the department. There was an insularity to this arrangement which guarded against fresh ideas and forward thinking.

Penhall's background saw him reduce important matters to the language of the book-keeper. In relation to the removal of 'half-caste' children into Colebrook Home he wrote: 'I hope this type of service may be increased. I consider the grown up aborigines more or less a liability, the children can become an asset.'[26]

Professor Cleland, the de facto chairman of the board, was also an arch-conservative in matters of Aboriginal policy. In 1966, with many years experience in Aboriginal affairs, he was to voice his opposition to having *any* land set aside for Aboriginal people[27], and in 1965 he argued that they could purchase their land like anyone else: 'They do this by the use of money which represents work done and not yet fully rewarded. The lands of Australia are open to such purchase by the original native inhabitants equally with the Europeans.'[28]

The pedantry of this passage is rivalled only by its lack of insight. Cleland appears to have been almost completely blind to the impediments to Aboriginal participation in the economy, society and politics of South Australia. This is unforgivable given his direct role in overseeing and maintaining these same impediments.

Born in 1878, and so 10 years older than Penhall, Cleland had a varied and distinguished career as a pathologist, physical anthropologist and botanist. At the time of his appointment to the board, Cleland was professor of pathology at the medical school at the University of Adelaide. In the late 1920s, he had become the chief blood grouper of the university's Board of Anthropological Research. In his travels throughout South Australia and the Northern Territory, 'Cleland never tired of bleeding Aborigines', even when the blood group data became predictable. His group 'gained the sobriquet of "the butchers" from the surrounding Aborigines'.[29]

Cleland was instrumental in having the medical card system in use at Point Pearce and Point McLeay extended to include social data. Early on in his term on the board he wrote:

> The proposed card index of all natives under the control of the Board, might include such items, as age, parentage, where located, mental ability, willingness to work, tidiness of the home, offences against the law, work and wages earned from time to time. In fact, all matters which may assist in the summing up of a person's activities both those favourable and unfavourable.[30]

While the card system was under construction, the primary tools used by the department to control behaviour were bluff and threat. Aboriginal fathers, for instance, were threatened with the removal of their children for omissions such as not regularly sending maintenance money to their families.[31] In March 1942, Penhall made an Aboriginal man's receipt of his deceased sister's estate contingent upon him requesting and receiving exemption from the Aborigines Act. Penhall wrote: 'I have to advise that there is provision under the Aborigines Act to administer your funds.'[32] Meanwhile, he admitted to his board: 'There is no power to retain the money without the consent of the aborigine concerned.'[33]

Penhall was not above invoking the spectre of the removal of their children to control certain Aboriginal people. In April 1941, he wrote to the wife of an Aboriginal serviceman:

> Do not be under any misapprehension about my ability to have your pension allowance reviewed by the Defence Department, and do not forget that your children are under the legal guardianship of the Aborigines Protection Board.[34]

Two months later, in relation to the same woman, Penhall advised the Swan Reach police:

> You will be interested to know that I spoke to Mrs. [Shepherd] regarding her manner of life when she was in Adelaide recently, and told her that, if she did not mend her ways, I would recommend the Board to take charge of her children. She begged me not to do this, and promised tearfully to mend her ways.
>
> If there is not a definite improvement I intend taking the action outlined above.[35]

Throughout his time as the administrative head of the department, Penhall kept a tight rein on the flow of information to his board, as we saw him foreshadow in 1938. When Mr Wyld, the missioner at Umeewarra Mission, three kilometres north of Port Augusta, asked to meet with the board, Penhall wrote:

> I shall be pleased to see you in town, and discuss with you any matters that you desire should be brought before the Board. It is not the practice of the Board to grant interviews at Board Meetings. All business affecting the Board is prepared and introduced by the Secretary.[36]

Penhall also made sure he kept a very low public profile. This kept the work of his department out of the public gaze. His only regular public engagement was to give a lecture in social organisation at the University of Adelaide every second year. When the university invited Penhall and his wife to attend the first screening of Charles Mountford's Central Australian films on a Thursday evening in late June 1941, Penhall gave his apologies.[37] This, as we shall see, was to become his usual practice.

On 9 December 1941, Lord Gowrie, the governor-general, issued a proclamation declaring Australia to be at war with Japan.[38] Black-outs were soon instigated at Point Pearce, with the windows of cottages screened prior to the lighting of lamps or candles.[39] Wartime restrictions were introduced with food, clothes, tobacco, liquor and petrol all being rationed.[40] Meat, butter, sugar and tea were rationed, with all except butter being part of the staple diet of Aboriginal people in South Australia at the time.

Factories at Wallaroo, Clare, Port Pirie, Mount Gambier and Lobethal made clothes for the armed services, and flax mills were established at Laura, Clare, Morphett Vale and Auburn.[41] Adelaide's perceived safety from a first strike on Australia, and its position roughly midway between the east and west coasts, meant that it was favoured by the program of decentralisation of munitions production under Essington Lewis, the Commonwealth Director-General of Munitions.[42] Munitions factories were established around the city.

During the war years, Aboriginal people experienced close to full employment in South Australia. Federally, this period saw the extension of the Commonwealth child endowment scheme to some Aboriginal families (1941), and access to pensions for some Aboriginal individuals (1942).[43]

Penhall was quick to take the side of mission authorities when they found themselves at odds with Aboriginal parents. In October 1942, Penhall was told that an Aboriginal woman wanted her daughters returned to her from Nepabunna Mission. Penhall advised her: 'Section 10 of the Aborigines Act makes the Board the legal guardian of all children under 21 years of age. You will see therefore that you cannot remove the children without the permission of the Board.'[44]

On the same day he advised Eaton, the missioner-in-charge at Nepabunna: 'If she applies to the Board I shall oppose the removal of the children, and I do not think the Board will allow it to be done.'[45]

However, Penhall knew that his authority to remove or withhold Aboriginal children from their parents in favour of private religious organisations was highly questionable. In March 1943, writing to a man who had asked him to help remove his son from his Aboriginal mother, Penhall wrote:

> The difficulty about the baby is that I cannot prove that [Ally] has neglected the child, or that she is not capable of caring for him. I will watch the situation carefully, and try to get [Ally] to agree to placing him in a Home. This is the only course open to me, as I could not succeed in any action through the Courts to take him away from his mother.[46]

A few months later, Penhall gave his commissioner a partial outline of the legal position of the board in relation to taking children. The commissioner requested this information following the 'agitations' of R.G. Campbell, a resident of Quorn and regular correspondent to Penhall on various subjects including police brutality towards Aboriginal people and 'neglected' children in the far north. Penhall wrote:

> The Aborigines Protection Board is the legal guardian of all aboriginal children under the age of 21 years by virtue of Section 10 of the Aborigines Act, 1934–39.
>
> In exercising the powers conferred by this Section, the Board seeks to maintain family life as far as possible. The extreme action of removing children from the custody of parents is taken only after the most careful enquiries provide substantial evidence of the inability of parents to control and care for their children.
>
> To remove children from a family circle is a serious matter, and, to avoid such action, every opportunity is given by the Board to aboriginal parents and guardians to exercise the privileges of parenthood in a satisfactory manner.[47]

Invocations of 'the most careful enquiries' and 'substantial evidence' were laughable. In fact, Penhall was very lax in his handling of child abuse investigations, often taking the uncorroborated word of a single white official as the basis for his decisions. In August 1942, Mounted Constable John Connell of the Oodnadatta police advised Penhall that his wife was willing to take in a 10-year-old Aboriginal girl, Louise, to train as a 'house girl'. He described her mother as having a 'vicious disposition' and little interest in her child.[48] Accepting Connell's assessment, apparently without further enquiry, Penhall wrote:

> I am very pleased to know that you are willing to have [Louise] for training as a house girl if her sight is restored. Apparently her mother is not a fit and proper person to have charge of the child.[49]

A similar incident occurred in May 1944, when Sister Phyllis McKenzie, the department's welfare officer, reported on the care of Ted Taylor's three children, living with a relative at Meningie. They were, she said, 'in a filthy condition'.[50] On the basis of this information alone, Penhall requested of the Meningie police that they encourage Taylor to place his children in the Colebrook Home.[51]

Mounted Constable McInerney then advised Penhall that Taylor rejected McKenzie's allegation, insisting that his children were 'warmly clad, well fed, and are quite happy under the care of Mrs [Keane] who is very much attached to them'. He added: 'He states that unfortunately Sister McKenzie saw them at a time when they had just previously been playing in the sand and paddling in the water.'[52]

Indeed, McInerney approved of Taylor's arrangement, noting that while they were at Meningie he had seen the children and their carer frequently 'and in fairness to Mrs [Keane] I feel that I must say that at no time during those months did the children give me the impression that they were neglected'.[53]

Penhall then withdrew his request, but the pattern was repeated a month later. Following her visit to Wudinna in June 1944, McKenzie reported that Mary Baker's house and children were 'dirty' and she could not pay her rent because her child endowment was not being sent on from Koonibba Mission.[54] Instead of asking the Koonibba authorities to send her the money they were collecting on her behalf, and *illegally* withholding from her, Penhall instead requested of the Wudinna police: 'I shall be glad if you will bring pressure to bear upon this woman to return immediately [to Koonibba] and, if necessary, provide her and the family with fares ...'[55]

Not known for his sympathetic treatment of Aboriginal people, Constable Veitch nonetheless defended Mrs Baker, reporting that she and her husband refused to return to Koonibba. He pointed out that when last they were there, they were given a two-room house to share with 12 people in all. He added: 'Mrs. [Baker] usually keeps her home reasonably clean, however it was unfortunate for Mrs. [Baker], as Sister's visit caught Mrs. [Baker] ill and confined to her bed, hence the children and the house had been neglected.'[56]

McKenzie had conveniently not reported this fact. Despite these failings of procedure, the annual report of the board for 1943/1944 noted:

> The Welfare Officer, Sister P.E. McKenzie, experienced a very busy year, travelling long distances, and making *careful enquiries* in practically every part of the State, regarding the physical, moral and social conditions under which the people live [emphasis added].[57]

As we have seen, Penhall was capable of threatening to remove children to secure changes in behaviour. The case of Mrs Ted Taylor demonstrates this. In July 1943, the superintendent of Point McLeay advised Penhall that Mrs Taylor had left her husband for another Aboriginal man, Malcolm Keane:

> [Taylor] says he will not take his wife back but he would like to have the boy and let his wife have the 2 girls. However, both the Police and myself consider this woman is not fit to bring up girls; therefore I suggest that the father has the eldest child – the boy – and the girls be taken from their mother.[58]

Penhall then suggested to the officer-in-charge of the Meningie police that it might be 'necessary' to cancel Keane's licence for his block of Coorong land, 'and issue it to some person more worthy'. He confided to the police officer that he wanted Taylor and his wife reconciled 'and the children kept together in the home'.[59] Dispossessing Keane of his land was apparently necessary to ensure that Mrs Taylor returned to her husband.

It is not clear whether this was carried out, but in any event the police officer 'returned' Mrs Taylor to her husband. He advised Penhall: 'she now appears to have received a thorough frightening and pleads to be allowed to retain custody of her children and states she will not err again.'[60]

In this same week, the ruling Liberal Country League party released an advertisement for the upcoming State election. It outlined eight principles for government action. The first four of these related directly to the war effort. The sixth principle was: 'The freedom of the citizen, his family, home and business from unnecessary controls, regulations and interference.'[61] Clearly, the principle did not apply to Aboriginal people.

The federal election in August 1943 gave the Labor Party 'an unprecedented triumph', delivering it 49 of 75 seats in the lower house and every contested seat in the Senate. On the back of this victory, John Curtin's Labor government requested that 14 powers be retained by the Commonwealth for five years after the end of the war. These were put to a federal referendum in August 1944 on an all-or-nothing basis.[62] One of the 14 powers was the control of Aboriginal affairs in Australia. Only the public of South Australia and Western Australia voted in favour and the referendum was rejected.

Meanwhile, the policies of the board were left to stagnate. The 11-point policy they introduced in 1941[63] was rarely acted on, let alone added to. The unpublished policy of the department continued to hold sway, the primary goal of which was to end the 'burden' of providing for Aboriginal people. To this end, assimilation was the covering ideology for a reluctance to properly fund Aboriginal development. The idea was to assimilate Aboriginal people into the community and so be done with them. It differed little from the 1930s notion of 'breeding the Aborigines white'.

This unpublished policy is found scattered throughout Penhall's writings. In June 1943, he advised a member of the Victorian public:

> I have to advise that there is nothing to prevent any aborigine being completely independent of the Aborigines Department, and the whole of the efforts of the Department are directed towards this end. Unfortunately many of them are quite content with their present standard, and will make no effort to achieve independence. I do not think complete independance [sic] will be possible in most cases until some action is taken by the Board to ensure that persons able to fend for themselves no longer have the opportunity of living on Mission Stations.[64]

In July 1942, Robert Richards, the leader of the opposition, suggested that members of the board were 'perturbed' that they were not permitted to discuss the workings and objectives of the board with the public. He put it to the commissioner, McIntosh, that the board had been directed along these lines. McIntosh denied this and told parliament that the board could release any information relating to Aboriginal affairs that it deemed proper to give.[65]

Meanwhile, though, Penhall continued to make it extremely difficult for interested and motivated people, let alone the general public, to inform themselves of the actual conditions under which Aboriginal people in South Australia lived, or the workings of his department. In late 1943, Penhall and Cleland were instrumental in denying the anthropologists Ronald and Catherine Berndt permission to enter Aboriginal reserves to conduct their investigations into Aboriginal social, cultural and economic life. They considered that the Berndts, who were to become highly distinguished and respected members of the international academic community, were 'not suitable persons'.[66]

In February 1944, when Kathleen Grimmett, of the League for the Protection and Advancement of Aboriginal and Half-Caste Women, requested material from the department's welfare officer, Penhall advised her that any such communication would have to go through him.[67] In the same year, he rejected two invitations to attend meetings by the Anthropological Society of South Australia, one of which was to include an open discussion on Aboriginal affairs.[68]

Aboriginal people were similarly barred from the machinations of their own administration. In May 1944, when an Aboriginal man requested to be present at a meeting of the board, his request was turned down.[69] Indeed, no Aboriginal person was ever allowed to present their case to, or even be present at, a meeting of the board during Penhall's 14-year reign as its secretary.

Under Penhall, the department specialised not so much in *taking* Aboriginal children, as in *withholding* the already institutionalised ones from their parents. In May 1944, Penhall rejected Peter McCormack's request for the return of his four children from Colebrook Home.[70] Three months later, Erskine, the secretary of the UAM, advised Penhall that Mr and Mrs McCormack had 'made appeals to certain Societies and individuals to aid them in getting their children from Colebrook Home'. Erskine himself recommended the release of the children 'in consideration of Mrs [McCormack] being a white woman'.[71]

Even in this unusual and politically sensitive case, Penhall was not to be dissuaded. He recommended to his board that McCormack's application be rejected and he be told to reapply at the end of the year.[72] The board approved this measure. Penhall then informed McCormack that his children would be released in December, provided he had renovated the house he was living in, furnished it, and settled his outstanding account with the UAM for the accommodation of his children, which then stood at £13, increasing by £1 per week.[73] The children were eventually released the following year.

In February 1945, Erskine advised Penhall that the UAM would take admissions into Colebrook Home only if the parents of the children signed a form providing that boys would stay until they turned 15 years of age; girls, 16.[74] In her account of her own childhood spent at Colebrook Home, Doris Kartinyeri includes the form that her father signed, giving her into the care of the UAM. It reads:

> Whereas I ____________ am desirous of giving my child ____________ into the care of the United Aborigines' Mission, Colebrook Home, until he or she reaches school-leaving age (16) and the above named Mission has found a situation for him or her.[75]

According to Kartinyeri, her father was led to believe he was merely signing a form to allow her to receive her child endowment benefit. This rings true, as the UAM generally required that the child endowment due to any child in one of their children's homes be transferred from the parents to them, supposedly to be spent on the child.

In late 1946, Erskine sent Penhall a copy of the form and requested a legal opinion on its validity.[76] Penhall took up the matter for the UAM, suggesting that the Crown Solicitor be asked to draft a suitable form of agreement. He noted:

> The attached copy of the agreement appears to have little value, and I doubt whether it could be enforced by legal action in the Courts, particularly as, under the provisions of Section 10 of the Aborigines Act, the Aborigines Protection Board is the legal guardian of such children.[77]

The Crown Solicitor was clearly not impressed with either the form or the request and said that he was not prepared to do the work that should be done by the UAM's own lawyers.[78]

After reading the Crown Solicitor's letter, Penhall advised Erskine that

> it is undesirable for agreements [for children to be placed in UAM homes] to be made irrevocable, but should be terminable at the will of the parents of the children concerned.[79]

This brought into question the methods of both the UAM and the Aborigines Department.

In May 1946, Penhall was again asked by his minister to explain the department's stance in relation to taking children from their parents – the minister having apparently received more complaints on this issue. Penhall again advised McIntosh that the Act made the board the legal guardian of every Aboriginal child until they reached the age of 21. He also noted that the only sections of the Act which spoke of committing children to institutions were sections 38, 39 and 40 – the old 'transfer of control' provisions of the discredited 1923 Act – under which Aboriginal children could be summarily committed to the Children's Welfare and Public Relief Board with the approval of that body. He proceeded to give McIntosh the official, politically palatable view of the actions of the department; a highly sanitised version of what it was doing. He wrote:

> The only conditions under which South Australian aboriginal children are removed from the care of their parents and placed in institutions are:
> (a) by agreement with the parents concerned that the child be placed in a Home established for the education and protection of aboriginal children.
> (b) by committal to the care and control of the Children's Welfare and Public Relief Board by action in the Children's Court ...
> (c) transfer by mutual agreement betweeen the Aboriginal [sic] Protection Board and the Children's Welfare and Public Relief Board.[80]

As the measures outlined in parts (b) and (c) were rarely if ever used by the department in relation to young Aboriginal children, most of the cases we have seen here appear to fall under part (a); that is, children were committed with the consent of their parents. He then made this assertion:

> During the many years I have been associated with the Aborigines Department, I cannot recall a single instance of a young child being placed in an institution by one of the above mentioned methods without the consent of the parents concerned. Many native parents appear to realise the need to provide a better environment for their children than that associated with native camps and cottages.

He went on:

> When a case of neglect of native children comes under the notice of a Police Officer, the matter is reported immediately to the Head of the Aborigines Department [i.e. Penhall himself], who details a lady Welfare Officer to investigate the circumstances under which the family lives, and, if the children concerned are obviously neglected or uncontrolled, arrangements mutually satisfactory to the Department and the parents are entered into for the admission of the children to a suitable institution. *It has not been found necessary to remove a child from the care of the parents without their consent* [emphasis added].[81]

Clearly, Penhall was capable of lying to his minister on an issue as important as the right of parents to the custody of their children. What chance did Aboriginal parents have in getting from him an honest appraisal of their rights?

CHAPTER FOUR

'All natives are liars', 1946–1949

'I AM NOT ASKING YOU MUCH. I NO [SIC] I HAVE DONE SIN, BUT I KEPT MYSELF STRAIGHT FOR NEARLY 6 YEARS NOW. I WILL BE QUITE LONELY IF YOU PUT THE THREE IN [UMEEWARRA MISSION].'

CAROL ANDERSON TO PENHALL, 24 FEBRUARY 1948, GRG 52/1/1948/1

During the early 1940s, four children's homes run by religious organisations were officially recognised by the Aborigines Department: the United Aborigines Mission's (UAM) Colebrook and Ooldea homes, and other homes at the Plymouth Brethren's Umeewarra Mission at Port Augusta and the Lutherans' Koonibba Mission. A fifth was added with the establishment of the Gerard Children's Home in 1946. In each of these, the children were at least partly maintained through the department by the issue of items such as food (flour, sugar, tea, cocoa, rice, split peas), soap, blankets, and clothing, and by a payment at the rate of five shillings per week 'when children are committed to the Home by the Aborigines Protection Board'.[1] Penhall championed the activities of these religious organisations:

> The organisations represented in the Homes under discussion are doing a wonderful work in this State, and the tendency is to increase the number of such Homes, so that the children whose living conditions are not ideal may be catered for and given a fair chance to make good.[2]

Throughout his reign, Penhall colluded with the authorities of religious missions in their attempts to control the behaviour of their Aboriginal residents. In October 1946, Andrew Pearce, the missioner-in-charge of the Finnis Springs Mission, suggested to Penhall that he intervene in the case of a young Aboriginal woman with a child:

> [Jacqui Kerr] seems rather independent & well off. So much so that she refuses to do a little washing etc for a few extra shillings. I wonder if you may feel it better to withhold your amount of £2 monthly from her. I feel she could manage without it.[3]

Pearce was referring to the child endowment money that Penhall administered on her behalf. Though he had no legal authority to withhold her child endowment, Penhall was happy to oblige this request. He wrote: 'In view of [Jacqui Kerr]'s attitude and apparent opulence I will not send any money for a time.'[4]

Penhall was also willing to use rations as an instrument of social control. In November 1947, he refused an unmarried woman and her child rations of food in order 'to [not] place a premium on wrong doing',[5] that is, in order not to appear to countenance childbirth outside marriage.

Penhall appeared to have a deep well of negativity from which to draw in his dealings with Aboriginal people. In August 1945, when the department's ex-welfare officer wrote to him with news of her work in the New Hebrides, Penhall responded:

> It must be very interesting work attending to the medical needs of the people. I hope they are less trouble and more responsive than the ilk we have to deal with. Sister McKenzie is still busy trying to make a silk purse out of a sow's ear, but feels that she is not making very much headway. The utter lack of co-operation on the part of the mothers and girls makes her work very difficult indeed.[6]

Penhall made his negativity and hardened attitude towards Aboriginal people plain to others he came into contact with. In April 1946, by way of introducing himself to the new officer-in-charge of the Wudinna police, Penhall wrote: 'I trust you will have a successful term of service at Wudinna, and will appreciate your co-operation in dealing with the very difficult problem of handling an unco-operative set of people.'[7]

A.H. Bray's attitude was equally bad. The ex-manager of Point Pearce, he had been called up for military-related duties in the early 1940s. He returned to the department in the newly-created position of Superintendent of Reserves, second-in-charge to Penhall. In January 1947, responding to the plan of a resident of Point McLeay Station to start a firewood business, he wrote: 'To me the whole proposition is the usual one from natives, they expect the whole outfit to be provided by this Department to start with, but are not prepared to start in a small way and build up.'[8]

In fact, the applicant, Johnson, had been providing firewood to residents of the station for some time. As a result of Bray's negativity, Johnson was denied a loan towards the purchase of a truck to cart the wood he cut. Undeterred, he made a success of the venture over the next 12 months, and, as a returned soldier, applied to the Repatriation Commission for funding. In September 1950, Penhall had to admit to Professor Elkin, head of the University of Sydney's Department of Anthropology, that Johnson had done 'remarkably well'.[9]

Penhall and Bray were not alone when it came to their attitudes. Almost all of the Aborigines Department staff had a negative attitude towards Aboriginal people. When Dr Ellice J. Davies was appointed as the department's inaugural welfare officer in early 1943[10], one of her first tasks was to visit the Port Augusta Reserve, where Aboriginal people were living in the sand hills near the town. She wrote: 'The people here seem of a degraded type, and the children, even very young ones, have already some very disgusting habits.'[11]

Dr Davies recommended a 'clean home' of 'orphan or unwanted babies' who can be brought up away from 'early habits' which she believed were a factor in 'the immorality of the dark people'. She also wanted a greater involvement in Aboriginal welfare by the Women's Christian Temperance Union.[12] Her replacement, Sister Phyllis McKenzie, the Point McLeay nurse, was overwhelmingly negative, and happy to continue the program of social control favoured by the department.[13] Doris Kartinyeri has written of Sister McKenzie's attempts to remove her from her father and extended family.[14]

In July 1947, McKenzie responded to a complaint from a young Aboriginal woman that she was made to work long hours for her employers and had to clean up after their dogs and goats, which were allowed to roam the house: 'As you know, all natives are liars unless it suits them to be otherwise.'[15]

From the evidence of her reports, McKenzie appears to have had an active dislike of Aboriginal people. In the mid 1950s, after Penhall had retired, she made it her business to keep the office secretary, a young woman with a keen interest in Aboriginal people, from talking to them.[16] When she reached her retirement age in March 1952, she was re-employed by the department after a week's break and continued on as their welfare officer.[17] The department could not bear to let her go.

There is a pattern in the attitudes of the staff of the department. Being a small one, its staff could be hand-picked for certain qualities. It appears they were, and that negativity and conservatism were two of the fundamental requirements. Compassion and empathy were clearly not valued. Such qualities were doubtless considered 'unpractical'.

As a result, the staff employed by the department did not reflect a cross-section of the general public. Indeed it becomes clearer, with each file read, that it was deliberately staffed in such a way as to *hamper* the social and political development of Aboriginal people. For many years, Penhall, McKenzie, and Bray happily assisted in a strategy of frustrating the legal and social ambitions of Aboriginal people in South Australia.

It is not that the standards operating in this era were so different as to preclude us from now judging the actions of the department and its staff. The department failed in its fundamental responsibilities, not only by our present-day standards but by those of its own era. Evidence for this comes in the form of occasional complaints about the administration, and the plight of Aboriginal people, made by various interested individuals. There would have been more of this but for the fact that complaint and dissent were stifled by the deliberate policy of limiting the information made available to the general public. Most South Australians simply did not know what was going on.

There were moments of charity though. In July 1947, Penhall sent blankets to two Aboriginal women living in 'a draughty cold tin house on the [Port Germein] reserve'. The normal issue was one blanket per person per year.[18] Penhall gave them two each.

Of course, Penhall was not responsible for the miserly financial regime he administered. That must be sheeted home to the Liberal Country League government, which was still no closer to presenting a new deal for Aboriginal people. In his pre-election policy speech of February 1947, Playford put forward, as he had done in 1941, four fundamental principles of good government. The third principle was 'to improve social services, public utilities and amenities, and to extend these even further into all parts of the State'. And yet, at the end of his speech, he said:

> Social questions are always ones upon which differing views will be held. My Government does not propose to introduce any major changes in the laws operating today, although action would be taken to meet any emergencies which might arise.[19]

So, the prevailing regime was to remain. There would be little extra spending on welfare until the economy was right. As with Playford's previous policy speeches, there was no mention of Aboriginal people.

Throughout the mid to late 1940s, the question of the Commonwealth assuming control of Aboriginal affairs was raised from time to time. Penhall blamed his board's failure to implement and develop Aboriginal policy on 'the lack of knowledge as to the intentions of the Federal Government in relation to future policy'. Because of this, he argued, no long-range policy had been developed. Finally though, in July 1946, he did concede that the issue needed to be resolved:

> It will be manifest, however, that such conditions cannot in fairness to all concerned continue indefinitely.
>
> The Aborigines Protection Board is desirous of the assistance of the Government in making an advancement in regard to native affairs, particularly because the absence of a definite policy of development is reacting very unfavourably on the natives.[20]

Penhall maintained that he had been led to believe, through conversations with the Commonwealth Director of Native Affairs, that the federal government would take control of Aboriginal affairs:

> However, month after month passes without any real evidence of this intention being given effect to. In the meantime, the conditions of the natives retrogress, and the Board is now faced with the situation that, unless some forward move is made, it will be forced to accept the responsibility for such retrogression.[21]

By January 1947, Penhall was advised that the Commonwealth would not seek a transfer of control of Aboriginal affairs.[22] This should have been the turning point in the revitalisation of Aboriginal policy in South Australia. It was not to be. And yet, in May 1947, Penhall submitted to his minister, for the first time, a list of proposed amendments to the Act which included:

- re-defining 'aborigine' to exclude a section of the Aboriginal community from the Act
- the control by the board of wages and working conditions of Aboriginal people in remote areas
- the licensing of employers of Aboriginal people
- the vocational training of 'suitable' Aboriginal people.[23]

But the real policy push continued to be that of the assimilation of Aboriginal people. The assimilationist, or 'absorptionist' program as it was sometimes called, turned in part on the issuing of exemptions from the Act. Penhall advised Premier Playford that it was the board's policy to establish 'suitable young mixed bloods, married or about to marry, in the general community', preferably in 'railway towns' with the men to be employed as fettlers:

> If financial assistance could be given to enable ten or twelve such young couples to be established each year in such a scheme, it would be a great help in absorbing the mixed bloods and relieving the problem of excess population on Mission Stations and in other institutions. Children of parents absorbed would then grow up in the general community, and would have no knowledge of Mission life ...[24]

Penhall continued to give short shrift to members of the public with an interest in Aboriginal affairs. In May 1946, a school headmaster from New South Wales informed Penhall that he was doing pioneering research on Aboriginal education and would be grateful if Penhall could have someone answer the questionnaire he had attached. This included questions on Aboriginal occupations, employment levels, occupational training, the development of Aboriginal skills, and his department's responsibility in relation to education.[25] Three weeks later, Penhall answered: 'I have been extremely busy, and, on account of the staff shortages, etc., have not been able to complete the questionnaire submitted.'[26]

It is highly likely that he could not complete the questionnaire because he had so little of the required information at hand. The department simply had no policy for the education and vocational training of Aboriginal children. Instead, he sent Beckenham copies of the department's annual reports of 1939, and 1942 to 1945, and also a copy of the Aborigines Act: 'you may be able to obtain from the reports a fairly comprehensive idea of the work being done in South Australia.'[27] Or maybe not. None of the information he sent gave the details Beckenham required. He had, of course, also failed to send him the 1941 report which outlined the policy of the board, such as it was.

The rest of the department was instructed to not answer public enquiries at all. In October 1947, acting secretary Bray advised the manager of Point Pearce Station to not respond in any way to a request from the Aborigines Advancement League for information on the 'industrial and technical training'[28] of young Aboriginal people for the monthly *Common Cause* newsletter.[29] The absence of such training had long been a sore point with the Aborigines' Friends' Association, and certain 'unpractical' members of the board.[30]

As we have seen, Penhall's position as secretary of the board gave him almost total control over the flow of information that the board received. Given that the board made many recommendations affecting specific Aboriginal people, Penhall had enormous power to affect lives. It is remarkable that, of Penhall's many hundreds of recommendations to the board, only one or two were amended before approval.[31]

In mid 1947, Dr Duguid resigned from the board, largely due to his frustrations with its conduct, its lack of capacity to effect change in Aboriginal affairs, and in particular its support for long-range weapon testing at Woomera. Just prior to this, Penhall had attempted to wrest the chairmanship of the board from Cleland. He had recommended that the Act be amended to make the secretary – himself – the chairman of the board.[32]

Cleland fought hard to counter this move. He clearly recognised Penhall's grab at power, and attempted to appease him in a report he made to the government:

> There have always been very happy relations between the Secretary and the members of the Board – the Secretary has been to all intents and purposes a member of the Board. I would suggest that he should be officially appointed as a member and that his administrative title should be, as it used to be, the Chief Protector of the Aborigines.[33]

Cleland was notably 'stiff and officious'[34], and his autobiography reveals a preoccupation with formality and a strong sense of being part of the Adelaide elite.[35] With Penhall willing and able to take on a man of Cleland's standing in a power struggle, it is not surprising that Aboriginal people who opposed Penhall stood very little chance of success.

In July 1947, E.P. Southwell, the missioner-in-charge of UAM's Gerard Mission, near Berri, wrote to Penhall. He asked Penhall to bring pressure to bear on Andrea Grant in order that her daughter, Susan, be kept at their newly established children's home.[36] Penhall readily agreed to do this. In fact, he recommended to his board that both Susan, aged seven, and Grant's other daughter Julie, aged 12, be held there. He wrote:

> Mrs [Grant] ... is not in my opinion a suitable person to have the custody of the older children. She was advised on several occasions not to leave the Gerard Mission, but she persisted in her intention to return to Swan Reach, where she has

> no means of sustenance.
>
> If Mrs [Grant] returned to the Gerard Mission, she would have access to the children occasionally, and will be provided with rations.[37]

If, in Penhall's opinion, Mrs Grant was not a fit person to have the custody of her children, the matter should have been referred to the Children's Welfare and Public Relief Board (CWPRB) in order that they could conduct an investigation, as per the report he made to his minister in June 1946.

For some years, Penhall had taken a hard line with Grant, a single mother, and denied her the assistance she needed to keep her family intact. In the winter of 1945, when requesting money from her child endowment funds to buy warm clothes for her daughters, she had written: 'I am on the sick list also my daughter [Julie] has been sick a good while now and also Mr Penhall I do need blankets badly I have only one and the nights are so cold ...'[38]

Even though all Aboriginal people were entitled to one blanket per year, Penhall's reply, in total, reads: 'In reply to your letter of the 17th inst., I have to advise that you have expended all monies received for Endowment, consequently I cannot accede to your request.'[39]

Miss Simmons, the missioner-in-charge of the Umeewarra Mission, was especially active in having Aboriginal children, in particular young Aboriginal girls, confined to her children's home. In October 1947, McKenzie reported: 'Miss Simmons is also hostile about children being taken out of the Home. She says that they put in a lot of hard work and see no results.'[40]

Penhall reassured Simmons on this point:

> I cannot agree to the removal of any of the children from the Home without the consent of the Board. After all you[r] work and trouble with little children it is not fair to you or to them that parents incapable of caring for them in infancy should have them later on and discount all the good work done. I suggest therefore that all applications for the release of children from the Home by [sic] made to you by parents in writing and referred to me with any comments you desire to make.[41]

Simmons's letters are full of appeals for her and Miss Cantle, her long-term companion and co-missionary, to be given custody of various children. In December 1947, she wrote:

> How do we stand in regard to Mrs [Belinda Duncan]'s children? They are such a

> bright, intelligent little pair, & coming along so nicely. We would gladly keep them altogether. Is that your intention? [Belinda Duncan] is at present either at Iron Knob or Whyalla. It was reported to me that she went to Whyalla with a certain white man. She does not appear to be a suitable person to have the care of children. The [Clark] children are very fond of fighting, & are not so attractive as their cousins, but they seem quite at home here. About [Fran Wilkinson]'s children, would it be possible to take them from her? We do not want them in our Home, unless necessary. I think they would be better right away.[42]

It must have been difficult for Penhall to know where to start with this breathless list of requests. In any case, he sent a telegram to the Wilkinson boys' guardian, Mrs Dickson, instructing her to place them in the children's home immediately.[43] She ignored this directive and it was left to McKenzie, using bluff and threat, the twin mainstays of the department's approach to Aboriginal people, to effect a result: 'Interviewed Mrs [Dickson] on arrival re placing [Mitchell] & [Sydney Wilkinson] in the Home. She was not in favour of this but, when told that the State Children's Dept. would take them if we did not, she agreed.'[44]

When bluff and threat failed, Penhall could withhold rations – as he did to Ruby Matthews and her young baby at Point Pearce Station. Penhall rejected Ruby's plan that she have her daughter cared for by her own family, to allow her to take up an offer of employment. The 'only possible course', Penhall wrote, was that Ruby's baby be sent to the Colebrook Home.[45]

In February 1948, Ruby's father took up his daughter's case. Matthews demanded of Penhall: 'do your Duty towards my Daughter [Ruby Matthews] & her baby Daughter By supplying them with food to eat …'[46] Penhall was dismissive:

> In case you may not know, I have to advise that all arrangements were completed some weeks ago between the Welfare Officer of this Department and your daughter, [Ruby], for baby to be placed in Colebrook Home, and for [Ruby] to proceed to a situation at Ardrossan …
>
> She has not kept her part of this arrangement.[47]

Clearly, Penhall was capable of applying severe financial pressure – to the point of denying food – to those Aboriginal people who did not comply with the removal of their children.

By contrast with the department, the CWPRB continued to treat Aboriginal people according to the rule of law. At various times during the 1940s, Aboriginal children were committed to the care of this board, often with little input from the department. Most of these children, however, were allowed to live with their families, under supervision.[48] The CWPRB preferred to work in a non-intrusive way with those Aboriginal families in which neglect was substantiated.

By May 1952, there were at least 25 children under the control of the CWPRB but living with their families at government stations, with the Aborigines Department reporting on the 10 children at Point Pearce and the 15 or so at Point McLeay. They were found to be 'all in good health, and reasonably well cared for'.[49] Tellingly then, in terms of retaining access to their children, having the CWPRB take them into their care gave a better result for Aboriginal parents than if the Aborigines Department had intervened.

In December 1947, a case emerged which would reveal the more enlightened approach of the CWPRB, and their general refusal to go along with the Aborigines Department's program of child removal. In this month, Penhall advised the manager of Point Pearce:

> I reported the misconduct of the [Anderson] family to the [Aborigines Protection] Board yesterday, and it was decided that Mrs. [Anderson] is not a fit person to have the charge of children. In consequence, arrangements will be made for [Lisa Anderson] and her young baby, and for [David], [Nancy] and [Carol] to be placed in the control of the Children's Welfare Department. Do not mention this to anyone at present. When the necessary arrangements are made, the children will be removed without notice or warning.[50]

The next day, he advised the CWPRB that his board had decided to commit the five Anderson children to an institution, subject to their approval.[51] He assumed the matter would proceed, for in an undated note, but presumably around the same time, he wrote that the children, aged from one month to 12 years, had been transferred to the CWPRB.[52]

An unpleasant surprise was in store for Penhall. In mid December, the chairman of the CWPRB advised Penhall that they would not approve the transfer of control of the children until the full facts of the case were submitted to them, nor until other avenues for the resolution of the issues were considered. He foreshadowed various problems with Penhall's proposed transfer:

> It is felt that the home standard required or accepted by an aborigine, would not be the same as that accepted for white children, and what would constitute neglect or unfit guardianship in a normal Australian home would not be regarded as such by a Magistrate in the case of aborigines, should the question of committal for neglect and unfit guardianship be a matter for decision by a Court.
>
> The Children's Welfare and Public Relief Board is aware that the moral code of aborigines differs from and cannot be compared with Australian whites ... This is a point for careful consideration in assessing the present conduct of the [Anderson] children.[53]

Penhall was clearly angered by the refusal of the CWPRB to back him up in this case. His memo to his board soon after, in which he called for four of the Anderson children to be immediately committed to the Umeewarra Children's Home, contains uncharacteristically abusive language. Still, the board approved his recommendation.

At the end of the month, the manager of Point Pearce warned Penhall that Mrs Anderson would call on him the following week 'with the object of retaining the custody of her children'.[54] It is not clear whether she did call on Penhall, as his office diary shows that he was in Canberra in the first week of February, attending the native welfare conference.[55] Three weeks later, Mrs Anderson reportedly agreed to take three of her children to the Umeewarra Home.[56]

She appealed directly to Penhall for the custody of her youngest daughter, wanting to keep her at home until she reached school age. On 24 February 1948, she wrote: 'I am not asking you much. I no [sic] I have done sin, but I kept myself straight for nearly 6 years now. I will be quite lonely if you put the three in.'[57]

Penhall immediately wrote to inform her that the board had made its decision and he had no power to alter it.[58]

Substandard health conditions endured by Aboriginal people directly affected their ability to retain the custody of their children. In January 1946, Penhall had requested the removal of a girl from Point McLeay to Colebrook Home on medical grounds. He advised the manager of the station that if her parents were unwilling to sanction this, the board would possibly act to remove them.

The girl in question, Thelma Reid, had been admitted to the Adelaide Children's Hospital some time prior to February 1945[59], for treatment for an acute hereditary disease. At the time she was eight years old. By February 1946, she had been transferred to Estcourt House, a convalescent home for children recovering from medical treatment, at Tennyson, on the Adelaide coast.

She was still there on 19 January 1948, on which morning her parents called on Penhall at his office, seeking her release. Penhall advised them to apply in writing to the board.[60] A few days later, her mother wrote:

> I am writing to ask if my daughter [Thelma] who is an inmate at the Estcourt House is in a fit state of health to return to us. It is over four years since she left home and we would very much like [her] to be with us again. At present we are at McLaren Flat and promise that we shall take every care of [Thelma] if she comes home. Thanking you for all that you have done for her.[61]

Penhall advised the board that, 'while sympathising with the mother', he recommended that she be told that it was 'in the best interests of Thelma if she remains at Estcourt House a little longer, particularly as she is doing so well at school'.[62] The board adopted this measure.

Later that year he sent Thelma's progress report from the Estcourt House school to the manager of Point McLeay:

> Please exhibit the report to the parents of this child and point out the great advantage she enjoys in receiving a good education.
>
> [Thelma] should not return to live at Point McLeay as in the atmosphere of the Reid home she would soon lose all the advantages gained by living in a decent place.[63]

The lack of rigour in child protection investigations and custodial deliberations continued to be a hallmark of Penhall's administration. In February 1948, Eve Gardner, of Anna Creek Station, died shortly after being admitted to Port Augusta Hospital, suffering from pneumonia. The doctor who attended her at the railway station at Hawker, 90 kilometres to the north of Port Augusta, refused to admit her to the hospital there 'owing to staff difficulties etc', which appears to have been a standard excuse used by certain members of the medical profession in South Australia at the time, to exclude Aboriginal patients. Eve was travelling with her husband and two children, a girl of two and a boy of four. Miss Simmons, of Umeewarra Mission, asked Penhall if she could take the children into her home. She made no mention of the father's wishes in this matter.[64] Penhall immediately replied:

> With regard to the death of [Eve Gardner], I am doubtful whether she would

> have survived even if she had been removed from the train at Hawker, although, of course, one cannot be sure in cases like this.
>
> I think it would be an excellent thing if the children could be placed in the Home, and I may state such action will be entirely approved in the interests of the children.[65]

The effects of the war lingered in South Australia. Though the rationing of clothing and meat ended in June 1948[66], any slight gains for Aboriginal people were quickly offset by the rising cost of food with rapid inflation.[67] Tea and butter continued to be rationed until 1950.[68]

Towards the end of 1948, a retirement from the board allowed Penhall to be unanimously appointed to the vacant position.[69] Now, in addition to being the secretary, he was a fully fledged member, with voting rights. Compounding the loss of Dr Duguid, the independence and strength of the board, such as it was, had been further weakened, as had happened to the Advisory Council of Aborigines before it.

An additional room was provided at the department's Kintore Avenue offices, to be used as Penhall's 'Office and Boardroom'.[70] Bray was made assistant secretary to Penhall and assumed some responsibility for decision-making.[71] He quickly flexed his administrative muscles, confining a young Aboriginal woman to Gerard Reserve in April 1949, and threatening another with the same treatment the following month.[72]

Despite his increased powers, but in line with his objective of keeping a very low public profile, Penhall declined almost every invitation made to him to attend public events in Adelaide in 1948, including a presentation by Mountford's research party to Arnhem Land, an invitation to meet the Mayor of London, an invitation to the Public Service Association ball at the Royal Palais, and a lecture by Dr Duguid.[73]

Penhall's determination to keep a low public profile had its corollary in his obsession with keeping the public away from Point Pearce and Point McLeay. In July 1948, he even rejected an offer from the Director of Agriculture for officers of that department to inspect the stations two or three times per year, to discuss and report on seasonal agricultural matters as they had done prior to World War Two.[74] He gave no explanation for this refusal.

He continued to block requests from interested groups, such as the Aborigines Advancement League, to visit the government stations.[75] By contrast, Penhall made his resources available at very short notice to a student of the Presbyterian Girls College at Glen Osmond, who was part of a team to debate with Scotch College on the subject 'The Australian Aborigine is justly treated by the White Australians'. Given the task of arguing in the affirmative, she requested from Penhall information as to the work of his department.[76]

Penhall replied:

> I think perhaps it would be advantageous for you to call at my office, if possible, armed with a series of questions to enable me to supply the answers you need. It might be also that I will be able to suggest certain lines of attack in the forthcoming debate.[77]

Two weeks later, the girl wrote back to Penhall, thanking him for his assistance:

> The information which you gave me proved of inestimable value. It gave me confidence and assurance to state my case, and although we did not win the debate the facts which you gave me enabled me to score top marks ...[78]

In the absence of any public scrutiny, Penhall could do as he wished. Not content to merely exert control over Aboriginal people, he even tried to control those who had been *exempted* from the Act. These people were legally members of the general public, their status as Aborigines having been revoked under section 11 of the Act. As such, they were not entitled to any assistance from the department, and did not come under the control of the board.

This was of little consequence for Penhall, who was concerned that some of these exempted people were cohabitating with Aboriginal people. Under section 85 of the *Police Act 1936*, it was still an offence for a non-Aboriginal person to cohabit with an Aboriginal person. In relation to the case of an exempted Aboriginal man living with other Aboriginal people, Penhall wrote:

> May I suggest that an opinion be obtained from the Crown Solicitor as to whether Section 85 of the Police Act, 1936 applies to [Shaw], and all other persons exempted by virtue of Section 11(a) of the Aborigines Act, 1934–39.
>
> It would appear that persons entirely exempted and living in the general community should not be permitted to lodge or wander in the company of aboriginal natives of Australia.[79]

As a result, the exempted man was successfully prosecuted by the Kimba police for a breach of the Police Act, one of the few such cases to be pursued by South Australian police in the twentieth century.[80] It is deeply ironic that it was an Aboriginal man who was so prosecuted.

Aboriginal people continued to be subjected to the extraordinary powers vested in the board. The board could hold Aboriginal people indefinitely at various locations around the state, without trial. Alternatively, it could exclude specific Aboriginal people from everything they held familiar and dear, also without trial, by expelling them from Aboriginal reserves. Both these powers were used many times by the board during Penhall's reign.

Some indication of the scope of these powers is given by the case of Peter Wallace, an Aboriginal resident of Point Pearce Station. In April 1949 he was informed that if he remained at the station he would be expelled. The manager there alleged that Wallace was the father of several illegitimate children and responsible for the pregnancy of Grace Reynolds. Wallace, he informed Penhall, would challenge any expulsion in court.[81]

In reply, Penhall noted that he had 'no actual proof' that Wallace was responsible for Grace Reynolds's condition and requested that they be 'kept under surveillance'. In any case:

> I am not concerned about any Court action [Wallace] might take, as he would be expelled under the regulation which gives the Board authority to expel persons whose presence on the Station is regarded as inimical to the maintenance of discipline and good order. Under this regulation no specific offence need be committed before action is taken.[82]

Despite such cases, Penhall still continued to show glimpses of a more charitable nature. He did what he could to help Ben and Beth Stewart, of Goolwa, with clothes, building materials, and other items. Close to pension age and looking after their grandchildren, they were both in very poor health, unable to work, and dependent upon Penhall's goodwill.[83]

CHAPTER FIVE

'If it would be a punishment', 1949–1953

'SHE HAS BEEN AWAY FROM US FOR SEVEN YEARS AND WE FEEL THAT WE HAVE THE RIGHT TO HAVE OUR OWN DAUGHTER HOME WITH US AT CHRISTMAS TIME ... I AS THE MOTHER OF [THELMA] IS PLEADING TO YOU. I AM ONLY ASKING WHAT IS RIGHTLY AND LEGA[L]LY MY OWN PRIVILEGE.'

MRS TIM REID, POINT MCLEAY STATION, TO PENHALL, 29 NOVEMBER 1950, GRG 52/1/1950/4

'THE ABORIGINES PROTECTION BOARD HAS NO POWER OR AUTHORITY TO REMOVE CHILDREN FROM THEIR MOTHERS, AND IN FACT HAVE NEVER DONE SO.'

PENHALL TO FREDA BROWN, BRONTE, NSW, 1 NOVEMBER 1951, GRG 52/1/1951/30

From late 1948 onwards, Penhall generally sought the approval of his board before committing an Aboriginal child to a children's home.[1] Prior to this he had often acted unilaterally, as if he were still the chief protector and the board did not exist. Indeed, it may as well not have, considering that among the many hundreds of recommendations for action that Penhall submitted to the board during the nearly 14 years he acted as its secretary, only one or two were rejected or even altered.

In January 1949, the case of Mrs Anderson and her children was raised again. In relation to the committal of three of her children to Umeewarra Mission, Penhall advised the manager of Point Pearce:

> You may give Mrs. [Carol Anderson] a fare to Pt. Augusta. Please advise her that her children in the Umeewarra Home are not to be interfered with in any way as they are to be kept there to give them a chance in life. If she does interfere she will be sent away from Pt. Augusta.[2]

When Mrs Anderson arrived at Umeewarra Mission with her baby, she found the rationing regime there quite different to that which existed at Point Pearce. She requested that her Point Pearce ration be reinstated.[3] Penhall replied ominously: 'I think you made a mistake in leaving Point Pearce Station.'[4]

He promised to look into the matter, but advised her that she would not be supplied on the same basis as she had been at the government station. Penhall then instructed Simmons to put Mrs Anderson on ordinary rations, with her baby to receive 'milk, semolina, etc'.[5] This 'ordinary ration' amounted to bread, tea, and sugar, and one shilling's worth of meat three times per week.[6] There was no provision for vegetables, fruit, or groceries. Clearly, there was a price for Mrs Anderson to pay if she chose to be near her institutionalised children.

As for Thelma Reid, of Point McLeay, her family continued to receive regular hospital reports of her progress. These were generally very brief, usually consisting of three words only – 'doing very well'.[7] At the April 1949 meeting of the board, her release from Estcourt House was discussed.[8]

By now, Thelma was 12 years old and had been at Estcourt House and in the Adelaide Children's Hospital since at least the age of eight. The next month, Penhall asked Pastor L.J. Samuels, the General Secretary of the United Aborigines Mission (UAM), if Thelma would be accepted at Colebrook Home 'as it is considered inadvisable to send her back to her parents'.[9] It appears that the action was somewhat rushed, as Penhall wanted her taken into Colebrook Home that same week, before his board could meet.[10] The transfer appears to have been effected without the sanction of the board. In September 1949, McKenzie noted:

> [Mary Reid] is perturbed as she has never heard from [Thelma] since she went to Colebrooke [sic]. [Mary] sent [Thelma] a cake for her birthday and she did not even thank her. Spoke to Miss Rutter and she said that they do not encourage the children to write home. I asked that [Thelma] be allowed to acknowledge her cake as she has hurt her mother.[11]

As usual, McKenzie's reading of the situation put the Aboriginal protagonist in the worst possible light. The fault lay with Thelma, not with the missionaries! Soon after, Mrs Reid again requested the release of her daughter into her custody. This followed the death of one of her other children. She wrote: 'This trouble I had upset all my plans so I want to live a quite [sic] life with my family. I am begging you Sir please don't disappoint.'[12]

Penhall wrote to the manager of Point McLeay: 'I sympathise with Mrs.

[Reid] in the loss of her child recently, but I think it would be a mistake to jeopardise [Thelma]'s chances of success by allowing the child to return to Point McLeay.'[13]

The manager of the station could not persuade Mrs Reid that it was in Thelma's best interests for her to remain at Colebrook Home. Mrs Reid had heard that Thelma was not attending dress-making classes as had been promised, but was instead working as a domestic servant at the home and doing 'the dirty work' there.[14] Penhall then rejected her request to visit Thelma at Colebrook Home: 'I think if [Thelma]'s mother came to town, she would do more harm than good so far as the welfare of the child is concerned.'[15] It is possible that he did not want her enquiring too deeply into the welfare of her own child.

In April 1949, the case of Mrs Andrea Grant again gained prominence. Southwell, the missioner-in-charge of Gerard Mission, alleged that Mrs Grant was having an 'adulterous' relationship. Even though she was living away from the mission, Southwell made the following suggestion:

> The difficulty is to know what punishment to give her [for adultery]. She has, up to date, desired to keep her child [Susan]. If it would be a punishment to her, I would say put [Susan] in an Institution for she is very dirty and neglected.[16]

Penhall immediately agreed to remove Mrs Grant's daughter, though he was careful enough to change the reasoning behind the move, from the punishment of the mother to the 'protection' of her daughter. On the same day that he received Southwell's letter, he wrote to Samuels:

> I have come to the conclusion that, for the welfare of the child, [Susan], she should be taken into the Home at Gerard. I shall be obliged if you will endeavour to arrange this, and report if the mother is unwilling.
>
> I should like to know also whether there are any other children in Mrs. [Grant]'s custody.[17]

But Penhall was clearly unsure of his exact legal position, for the following month he requested a report from the Crown Solicitor 'as to the powers of the Aborigines Protection Board in the matter of removing aboriginal children from the control of incapable and neglectful parents otherwise than by the method described in section 38 of the Aborigines Act'.[18] This section contained the 'transfer of control' provisions between his board and the Children's Welfare and Public Relief Board (CWPRB) – the discredited 'dead letter' provisions of the 1923 Act, which were rarely, if ever, used.

Penhall wanted to know especially whether action could be taken under sections 7(e), 7(g) or 10 of the Aborigines Act. The first two related respectively to the board's duty to provide for the custody, maintenance and education of Aboriginal children, and to exercise general supervision and care over all matters affecting the welfare of Aboriginal people.

Hannan, the Crown Solicitor, said that in his opinion, sections 10 (which made the board the guardian of all Aboriginal children) and 17 (which allowed the board to confine any Aboriginal person to any Aboriginal institution) could be used together to confine any Aboriginal child to an Aboriginal institution, 'without the consent of the child's parents'. But 'further than this', 'I do not think the Board has any powers in the matter' and sections 7(e) and 7(g) were 'not ... specific enough to authorize the removal of aboriginal children from their parents'.[19]

On the face of it, this advice appears contradictory. The Crown Solicitor suggests that the sections of the Act relating to guardianship and to committal *could be* used to confine a child to an Aboriginal institution. But then he appears to backtrack by noting that *further than this* the board has no power in the matter. Why was anything *further* needed? Would action under sections 10 and 17 somehow *not* constitute a legitimate removal of an Aboriginal child from neglectful parents?

It is possible that Hannan believed that a legitimate removal could only occur under the discredited and rarely used 'transfer of control' provisions of the Act, and that to use any other part was against the spirit of the Act. That is, while a child could be confined, say, to Umeewarra Mission without the consent of the parents, it could not be done on the grounds of neglect, and it could not be done indefinitely.

In any case, it appears that the department had been put on notice that much of what they had been doing in relation to the removal of Aboriginal children was of questionable legality.[20] Two years later, Penhall would deny that his board had ever removed Aboriginal children from their parents:

> The Aborigines Protection Board has no power or authority to remove children from their mothers, and in fact have never done so. Whenever children of aboriginal descent in South Australia are neglected or ill-treated, action is always taken by the Children's Welfare Department in the same way as that Department deals with neglected white children.

> A number of children are placed in special institutions by the Board for training, but this is only done with the consent of the parents.[21]

Before the opinion of the Crown Solicitor reached him, however, Penhall attempted to remove Susan Grant from her mother. He sent welfare officer McKenzie, who found Mrs Grant adamant that no one would take Susan away from her. According to McKenzie, Mrs Grant was 'most insolent and told me several times that it was none of my business how she lived'.[22]

A few days later, when Southwell visited Mrs Grant in order to take Susan from her, Mrs Grant again refused to hand her over. Southwell reported:

> As arranged by Sister McKenzie I called for [Susan Grant] yesterday but [Andrea] would not give her up.
>
> I reminded her that she was breaking her own promise & that it would mean police action having to be taken against her. She claimed that she was looking after [Susan] properly & that she wanted to know what [Brad (her husband)] thought of her parting with [Susan].[23]

At the next meeting of the board, Penhall requested that they commit Susan to the children's home at Gerard. He described Mrs Grant as 'a grossly immoral person' and noted that she was living in a tent near the packing shed at Berri. He requested that Susan be 'removed' from her and 'placed in the [Gerard] dormitory and kept there during the pleasure of the Board'. The board adopted this recommendation.[24]

The next day, Penhall advised Mrs Grant to hand Susan over to Southwell immediately, informing her that this was what her husband wanted her to do, a claim which appears to have been quite possibly false.[25]

When Southwell called on her a week later, she again refused to hand over her daughter, with Southwell reporting:

> I then told [Andrea] that I would call again on Monday & that if she did not hand over [Susan] then I would not call again & she must take the consequences. She replied that she was quite prepared to take them.[26]

The threat appears to have worked, however, for a few days later, Andrea handed Susan over to Southwell.[27] On 1 August 1949, Southwell reported: '[Susan Grant] has settled into Dormitory life & [Andrea] has been down twice to see her.'[28] Penhall responded: 'I am very pleased that Baby [Grant] has settled in to the dormitory life, and I think it would be a tragedy for [Andrea] ever to have control of these children again.'[29]

In the midst of all this, Penhall wrote: 'The Board should endeavour to keep the family unit intact, and, where this is not possible, make provision for the care and training of its charges.'[30]

Of course, the board did at times remove some Aboriginal children who appear to have genuinely been at risk of harm.[31] More often though, there was a capricious element to their removal, with such action precipitated by considerations apart from the protection of children, including the lifestyle of the parents, and whether or not the family or the child were deemed a 'nuisance'.

Meanwhile, Aboriginal policy continued to stagnate. In March 1949, when the secretary for the minister requested of Penhall the details of any new legislation required[32], Penhall replied:

> I do not know whether the Honourable the Minister of Works intends to proceed with a review of the Aborigines Act during the impending session of Parliament. I think it probable that the matter will remain in abeyance a little longer.[33]

As we have seen, Playford's Cabinet was made up almost entirely of ministers representing rural South Australia.[34] In the Legislative Council, the bias towards country and Liberal Country League representation was even more pronounced 'as a result of a property franchise and voluntary voting for that chamber'.[35] The chances of reforming the Aborigines Act, given that any such reform would require fundamental changes to the conditions of Aboriginal employment in the pastoral industry, were thus very slim.

In June 1949, with pressure from Aboriginal interest groups mounting, Penhall reminded his minister of the board's official policy, as outlined in the annual report of 1941. Virtually none of the 11 points had been attended to. Despite the Aborigines' Friends' Association (AFA) having pressed for years for vocational training to be set up at the government stations, nothing had happened. While a few Aboriginal men had found work with government departments such as railways and public works, there was grossly substandard housing at Point Pearce and Point McLeay, and little or no development of these or other Aboriginal reserves. The medical survey was a sham, and improvements to the ration scale, though long sought after and needed, were glacial in both speed and comfort.

As was his custom, Penhall deflected criticism of the board's inaction by blaming the victims of such inaction:

> It will no doubt be realised that the Board is able to implement its policy only with the willing co-operation of the people under its care, for instance, considerable difficulty is encountered in the matter of vocational training.[36]

Given Penhall's religious background, it comes as no surprise that one of the few policies of the board that Penhall actively sought to implement was that of devolving responsibility for Aboriginal people to religious organisations. As early as December 1940, Penhall confided to his counterpart head of Aboriginal affairs in Brisbane that his department planned to encourage religious organisations to take over the running of the Point McLeay and Point Pearce stations.

In November 1950, Mrs Reid, of Point McLeay, again pleaded for the return of her daughter for Christmas:

> She has been away from us for seven years and we feel that we have the right to have our own daughter home with us at Christmas time ... I as the mother of [Thelma] is pleading to you. I am only asking what is rightly and legal[l]y my own privilege.[37]

Penhall recommended to his board that, subject to the approval of the United Aborigines Mission, Thelma be permitted home for two weeks:

> ... whenever she has been permitted to return home and comes into contact with other children at the Station, and is treated in an unkindly way by them, her condition deteriorates. For this reason, all previous requests for the child to go home have been resisted.[38]

It is unclear on what basis Penhall made this assessment. The records suggest that Thelma had not been home for seven years. Thelma returned to Point McLeay and stayed there. McKenzie reported in January 1951:

> Interviewed [Mary] and [Tim Reid] concerning [Thelma]. (They had promised to return her to Colebrook Jan. 2.) [Mary] said that they were cruel to [Thelma] at Colebrook. (Don't believe this). Anyhow they could not be persuaded to let her go ...[39]

In January 1951, Penhall received medical advice regarding an infant, Paul Hurst. According to a doctor, his recurring bouts of sickness were 'due to neglect on the part of the mother, and wrong feeding'. Mrs Hurst was unwilling to place her son in the Umeewarra Home. Penhall wrote: 'Actually, the Board has not the power to remove the child from the custody of the mother, except through the Children's Welfare Department.'[40]

Not willing to refer the child to that department, he instead offered the following plan:

> Will you please ask Dr. Thompson if the child's condition warrants it being sent to Adelaide for further treatment. If such proves to be the case, the child could be brought down and kept here as long as possible, by which time probably the mother would have forgotten all about him.

It was essentially the same strategy he had attempted for Thelma Reid. He would make it harder for Mrs Hurst to refuse by threatening her:

> If Mrs. [Hurst] is still unwilling to place the child in a Home, then perhaps you could advise her that, if the child is taken ill again as a result of neglect or wrong feeding, I will ask the Board to take it away from her, and place it under the care of the State.[41]

The plan was put into action and Paul Hurst was committed to Colebrook Home in early February 1950.[42] McKenzie visited Mr and Mrs Hurst at Port Augusta a month later. She reported:

> [Sean (a relative of Mrs Hurst)] had written saying that [Paul Hurst] was fretting at Colebrook and he thought they should take him away. Explained that he was quite happy when I saw him but [Craig Hurst] [i.e. the father] thought he would go down next month and get him. Rang Miss Rutter and she said that [Paul] is perfectly happy and running about all over the place.[43]

This was little comfort to Mrs Hurst, who wrote to Penhall in late May 1950, concerned about her baby and wanting him returned: 'It's time I ought to have my baby home by now. I have been longer without him [than with him]. And I am quite worried about him.'[44]

From her letter, it is clear that no one had bothered to tell her that the department's intention was to withhold her child from her indefinitely. There is little else on file. Following her visit to Port Augusta on 30 May 1950, McKenzie reported that both Mrs Hurst and Joy Watson, a family friend, had asked for Paul to be returned home. She offered the following as reason for not returning Paul: '[Paul] is reported to be doing very well and as Mrs [Watson] and [Alison Hurst] have white men from the town visiting them at night his home life could not be satisfactory.'[45]

She offered no evidence for this assertion other than that Miss Simmons had claimed that unknown white men had been seen at the Umeewarra Mission on three occasions in the recent past. Five months later, McKenzie sent the following message to Craig Hurst, in full: 'Your son [Paul Hurst] is doing very well at Colebrooke [sic] Home, he is in good health and running about very happily. You need have no fear that he will be handed over to [Sean Watson].'[46]

The reference to his son not being handed over to a relative was simply an obfuscation to distract attention from the fact of Paul's detention. Two years later, Paul Hurst was still institutionalised – one of 45 Aboriginal children at Colebrook Home in 1952.[47]

The department's laxity in relation to the investigation of alleged child neglect continued to be a hallmark of its operations. In mid May 1951, Samuels, the UAM's general secretary, requested that an Aboriginal child at the Oodnadatta Children's Home be given into the care of a white family as he had no mother and 'I don't think the Father cares much about him'.[48] The day after receiving this, and apparently with only this rather vague accusation to go by, Penhall recommended to his board that the child be discharged from the Oodnadatta Home and placed with the family.[49] As usual, his recommendation was accepted without further enquiry.

Neither did Penhall offer any assistance to Aboriginal people whose children were being illegally detained by religious organisations. In early 1952, Jill Taylor, of Winkie, approached the superintendent of the Gerard Mission, requesting that her son be released from there. He had been there for 14 months. The superintendent told her that she needed Penhall's permission in order to remove her child.[50] When she wrote to Penhall he advised her that as the original arrangement was made with the UAM, the decision as to the custody of her son rested 'with the Mission and yourself'.[51] It didn't; it rested solely with Mrs Taylor, as Penhall knew.

Penhall could have told Mrs Taylor that she was free to take her son from the mission. To have done so in this case, though, may well have constituted a critical first step in a new regime of openness and honesty, in which Aboriginal people were made aware that they had the same rights to the custody of their children as enjoyed by the rest of the South Australian population. It could have been the first step in the dismantling of the board's actual power. Penhall was clearly unwilling to take such a step.

Indeed, the withholding from Aboriginal people of a frank and honest account of their legal rights was a key part of Penhall's strategy, repeated time after time. His failure to act here in the interests of the legal rights of Aboriginal people constitutes another violation of his and the board's role. Under section 7(g) of the Act, the board had a duty 'to exercise a general supervision and care over all matters affecting the welfare of the aborigines, and to protect them against injustice, imposition and fraud'. It appears that Penhall did not consider that this part of the Act applied to the board itself.

Why were religious organisations so ready to interfere in the relationship between Aboriginal people and their children? Could it have to do with the fact that they benefited financially from their illegal holding of Aboriginal children? In June 1953, welfare officer McKenzie advised the wife of a station manager that an ex-inmate of Colebrook Home would be sent to her to work as a domestic:

> She has been at Kolendo with Mrs. Brennan and there received 45/– a week. They [i.e. the UAM] think she is now worth 50/– per week — 10/– a week to be given her and £8/–/– a month sent to United Aborigines Mission, 66 Pirie St. Adelaide. When she requires clothing she can write them.[52]

So, as well as receiving an Aborigines Department subsidy and Commonwealth child endowment for each child in their homes, the UAM took eighty percent of their wage when they were sent out to work.

In March 1952, Penhall advised his minister, as he had every year, that 'it is not proposed to amend the ... Act ... during the next session of Parliament'.[53] The suggestion of legislative reform hinted at in 1947 had come to nothing. As far as the government and the department were concerned, the debilitating and corrosive conditions confronting Aboriginal people were incidental to the running of the state.

In January 1953, at the request of his minister, Penhall prepared an outline of his department's major activities for the past three years, and suggestions for future policy. The material was intended for use by the premier in his government policy speech.

Penhall listed four major projects – the acquisition of land at Point McLeay,

Ceduna, the north-west Reserve and Yalata Station; grants to missions; grants for Aboriginal housing; and the installation of irrigation equipment at Point McLeay.[54] His suggestions for future policy, his 'Forward Programme' as he called it, centred in great part on improvements to buildings and infrastructure.

Bereft of informed policy, it stands as a lasting indictment of Penhall's administration, revealing the department as almost entirely lacking in imagination or commitment. In May 1953, in what was Penhall's final opportunity to put forward *any* legislation during his time as the secretary of the board, he advised his minister: 'it is not proposed to make any amendments to the Aborigines Act during the ensuing Parliamentary Session.'[55]

The board, in its first 14 years of operation, had failed to make any contribution to legislative change in Aboriginal affairs in South Australia, despite being well aware of such things as gross violations of the rights of Aboriginal pastoral workers.

Like the politicians he served under, Penhall demonstrated an inflexible and almost wholly unimaginative character throughout his appointment as the head of the department. The latter is demonstrated by his constant failure to sympathise, let alone empathise, with Aboriginal people, or appreciate the harsh socioeconomic conditions they lived under. Though there were moments of generosity in his dealings with Aboriginal people[56], Penhall failed to uphold key responsibilities in relation to his duties as chief protector and then as secretary of the board – most notably the duty 'to exercise a general supervision and care over all matters affecting the welfare of the aborigines, and to protect them against injustice, imposition, and fraud'.

Penhall retired from the public service on 18 August 1953.[57] It was a watershed; the end of an era. At the end of the same month there was a meeting in the Adelaide Town Hall, organised by the Aborigines Advancement League and chaired by Dr Duguid, at which 'part-Aborigines' were to discuss the topics 'Our place in the community' and 'Why we need a hostel'. There were to be 'musical items by part-Aborigines', and the premiere of the film 'Men of the Mulga'.[58] It was the first time such a meeting had taken place in any town hall in a capital city in Australia.[59] Despite the spoiling work of Penhall and his department, there was a residue of social activism among the Aboriginal people of South Australia.

Aborigines Advancement League

Town Hall, Adelaide

Monday, 31st August

8 p.m.

Part - Aborigines will discuss

"Our place in the Community"

and

"Why we need a Hostel"

MUSICAL ITEMS BY PART - ABORIGINES

— and —

Premiere of

"Men of the Mulga"

(Colour Sound Film of Tribal Aborigines in South Australia's Nor'-West)

Chairman - - Dr. Charles Duguid

Admission: 2/-

PROCEEDS IN AID OF HOSTEL FUNDS

Tickets at Allan's, Rundle Street

Honorary Secretary: MISS FAITH HOLLIDGE, 24 Westall Street, Hyde Park

Specialty Printers Limited, 155 Waymouth Street, Adelaide.

CHAPTER SIX

'Our girls for slaves', Koonibba Mission, 1936–1952

'THE ULTIMATE AIM IS TO PLACE HER WITH A WHITE FAMILY.'

PENHALL, NOTE, GRG 52/1/1939/71

As oppressive as the United Aborigines Mission regime was, it was as nothing compared to that of the Lutheran Church's Koonibba Mission. Approximately 40 kilometres north of Ceduna, on the west coast of South Australia, it was far enough from civilisation to allow its staff to treat Aboriginal people as if they were without any rights at all. Penhall colluded with the mission authorities to systematically deny Aboriginal people the custody of their children. An examination of the historical records shows clearly his use of threat, bluff and lies to achieve this.

Koonibba Mission was established in June 1898. At the time, pastoral stations in the area were being converted to smaller, agricultural blocks. This put pressure on Aboriginal people, who were already competing for resources with pastoralists, and coming into conflict with authorities in small towns such as Penong and Fowlers Bay.[1]

The mission soon took over the task of distributing rations to the young, elderly and the sick. Early on, however, the Aboriginal camp 'remained physically and ideologically separate' from the mission, and was 'a refuge where people were able to maintain their own social and cultural forms'.[2] In return, the mission benefitted from cheap Aboriginal labour. By 1900, the farm overseer at

Koonibba 'had the highest return from scrubland of any farmer in the district', with 600 acres of land cleared.[3]

While early relations between the Aboriginal residents of Koonibba and the mission authorities appear to have been quite good, a petition during World War One, signed by 29 Aboriginal men, hinted at unrest. The petitioners requested that the mission be removed from 'German control' and placed under 'English Government control'.[4] The arrival of Pastor R.K. Traeger in the 1930s would heighten some of these tensions.

In January 1936, Matthew Lawson, an Aboriginal resident of the mission, asked Chief Protector McLean whether his people were under the control of the 'English Government' or the Lutheran Synod. He made a serious complaint that McLean could not ignore:

> can this mission authorities. controled our girls or boys. when girls or boy reaches their age 16 years or 18 years old. where they think. best to their own german people. them to use our girls for their slaves. without girls fathers consent.[5]

The charge was that the Koonibba authorities were placing Aboriginal children in domestic service, to members of the Lutheran community, without the consent of their parents, and for little or no remuneration. From the perspective of Matthew Lawson at least, the Koonibba children were being treated as slaves. At the time, four boys and 17 girls from Koonibba were with various Lutherans throughout South Australia and Victoria, working as domestic servants.[6] Lawson raised many issues in his letter, including that of parental consent, the children's wages, the lack of visitations allowed by both parents and children, and the lack of opportunity for children to lodge complaints against their employers. McLean confided to Pastor Traeger, the superintendent of Koonibba Mission:

> Although I have often discussed this scheme with you and Pastor Hoff I have never had anything in writing concerning the arrangements with employers and as the matter is occasionally referred to I would like to have something definite to work on.[7]

Traeger's response was simply to give the Aborigines Department more warning of the occasions when children were removed to work as domestics. In August 1936, he wrote: 'As we have an over supply of big girls in our Home, I would ask you to sanction that [Deborah Doyle], [Lisa Reynolds], and [Audrey Baker] be sent to Tarrington [in Victoria].'[8] He claimed that the girls had consented to go, and made it clear that the 'supply of big girls' was linked to the mission's financial obligations, with their removal being part of an arrangement with their backers: 'I am particularly anxious to fill this request as the Tarrington people are among the chief financial supporters of our mission. Care has been taken to choose three of our best girls.'[9]

McLean raised no objection to this arrangement, even though there was no information supplied on who the girls would work for, and the conditions they would face. It is clear that in his duty as chief protector, he should at least have investigated Lawson's claims that the children were being removed without parental consent.

In 1938, the case of 11-year-old Justine Reynolds was referred to McLean. McLean asked Traeger whether it would be in Justine's interest for her to be returned to her mother, Mrs Grace Sampson, of Point Pearce Station.[10] Traeger opposed this course of action, and McLean advised the superintendent of the station: 'it would be in the best interests of the child [Justine] for her to be taken into the Children's Home at Koonibba and trained until 14 years of age, then to be sent out to work.'[11] According to the superintendent, Mrs Sampson agreed that her daughter could stay at Koonibba until she had completed her religious confirmation, 'but hopes that you will then assist her to get the child home'. The superintendent argued: 'I am still of the opinion that this woman is entitled to have her daughter home with her.'[12]

At the same time, Traeger argued that Mrs Sampson 'did nothing to rear the child' and that Justine should not be given back to her. He dismissed another Aboriginal woman, who had written a letter supporting Mrs Sampson, as 'a mischief maker'. Traeger argued that Justine should be put into the Koonibba Children's Home until the age of 15 and then sent out to work: 'She is a very pale quarter caste and would feel at home and will be welcomed by whites.'[13] Penhall, by now the acting chief protector, agreed that Justine would stay at Koonibba Mission until she had completed her confirmation.[14]

In November 1938, Mrs Sampson again took up the issue, this time with Penhall: 'I would like you if possible to get my daughter over here before Christmas. I understand that the pastor over on Koonibba wishes her to complete her religious training under his care which will mean another two years.'[15]

Mrs Sampson told Penhall that a local Lutheran pastor had agreed to attend to Justine's religious training if she returned to Point Pearce. Penhall advised Traeger of this arrangement and ended his letter: 'I am sure public opinion would be opposed to the prolonged separation of the child from her mother unless it can be shown that the mother is incapable of caring for her.'[16]

Traeger still refused to release Justine. In May 1939, Pastor Hoff, the secretary of the Lutheran Synod, requested that Justine be kept at Koonibba Mission until the end of the year.[17] Penhall had just returned from a visit to Point Pearce where Mrs Sampson had 'made a strong appeal for the return of her child'.[18] Penhall told Hoff that she was well respected at the station, and 'no court would hesitate to give the mother custody of the child'. Still, he agreed that the request that Justine remain at Koonibba until the end of 1939 was 'a reasonable one', and he informed Mrs Sampson that Justine would be returned to her at the end of the year.[19]

Penhall did not keep his promise. In October 1939, he advised Mrs Sampson that Justine would now not be returned to her after all. He claimed to have seen Justine on a visit to Koonibba and 'she expressed a strong wish to remain at Koonibba'.[20] Mrs Sampson was indignant: 'I insist that you make her come here to where I am, I'm her mother; she is under age, she [h]as been influenced, led by others to resist my request; I want her to be here.'[21]

Penhall's response was blunt and unsympathetic:

> I pointed out that you are her real Mother but she said she had no desire to go to live with you and would not go unless I compelled her to do so.
>
> My advice to you is to accept the situation as it is just now and think of your Daughter as being happy where she is for the present.[22]

Penhall made no mention to Mrs Sampson of his plans for her daughter, confiding in an unsigned, handwritten note of his visit to Koonibba of 18 October 1939: 'The ultimate aim is to place her with a white family.'[23]

At this time, in August 1939, another Koonibba resident complained to Penhall that every time she needed her daughter's help with her housework she had to 'send a note to the Children's Home, or to the Superintendent'.[24] On a daily basis, that is, Mrs King had to make written application for the short term release of Wendy, aged 17, from the home. Previously she had made arrangements with the mission board for her daughter to visit her every day and 'sleep up [at] the Children's Home', but Pastor Traeger had ignored this. She wrote of Traeger: 'A person can lay here & die. He'll only know when to bury us. He doesn't care how we get on. Thats how Christianity is shown. By putting people Low & chucking dirt on us.'[25]

All of the white mission staff had access to Aboriginal domestic help, heightening her frustration at not being able to have her own daughter help her out. Worse still, a crippling foot condition meant she had to rely on other people for things as basic as fetching water and taking messages to Traeger. The visiting doctor had recommended special shoes for her feet, and while they were supposed to be ordered before the previous Christmas, Traeger had done nothing.[26]

Mrs King was clearly angry with the mission authorities for separating her from her children without her consent:

> they waited till I grew them up & went & shuffed them into the Children's Home, without letting a woman know anything about it, & promising me that if I [were] to live on this Mission like other Women, I could have my children.[27]

Her rations were stopped whenever she had complained about her treatment, and Traeger had told her: 'that in the whole world, that we never get [Wendy] [back]. We can write no matter to whom & there will be no notice taken.'[28] Having left the mission at one point with her daughters, she had been promised custody of them if she returned: 'this I did, but my children were never given back to me, till this day, & this has been driving me nearly an insane all these years, illness & one thing [and] another.'[29]

Mrs King's eldest child, Catherine, had been placed in the Salvation Army Home in Adelaide and then 'went out on Service to German Families to work for almost nothing while she was in ill-health': 'my heart-breaking she got married & had a child. I knew nothing of it because the German people brought her up not to have any respect to her mother.'[30] Penhall visited Mrs King in October 1939, found her request a reasonable one, and advised her that Wendy could return to her home.[31]

Two months later, Mrs King had to request permission of Penhall to go on holiday to Ceduna with her husband and daughter. She was reduced to asking permission, she explained, because Traeger had been 'slinging off' at her ever since Penhall's visit, telling her she had to write to Penhall for permission whenever she wished to do or have anything, even to go on holiday with her family.[32] She also requested of Penhall rations for the holiday period, noting that in previous years Traeger had refused to provide her with such.

Tying people up in red tape was one of Traeger's favourite strategies in making life difficult for those Aboriginal people who opposed his authority. Penhall was generally a willing participant in this. Now, he colluded with Traeger by telling Mrs King that the agreement that had been reached was that Wendy was allowed to live with her only 'on condition that the family remained at Koonibba'.[33] Effectively then, it appears that they were banned from leaving the mission. There was no legal authority for this. Penhall told her to take his letter to Traeger, and with his (Penhall's) permission they could take Wendy from Koonibba to Ceduna for a week or two. Penhall made no suggestion as to how she could get rations from Traeger, and made no intervention on her behalf.

According to Mrs King, Traeger had certain favourites among the Aboriginal residents of Koonibba, and those who were out of favour with him were victimised. Though she had been requesting a water tank for several years, hers was the only cottage without one. Her foot condition meant that it was left to her youngest daughter to cart water. It appears that Traeger favoured those Aboriginal people who were quiet and made no trouble for him. Mrs King wrote:

> We are not so bad as what these evil-minded people, who are not clear in their senses, think & to look down on some people, who they don't like. Who they don't like, is the onces [sic] who speaks the Truth.[34]

In early 1940, Penhall drafted an undated minute to his board[35], advising them that Mrs Sampson had again made application for the custody of Justine, now aged 13. He recommended that her request not be granted and that she be advised to apply again at the end of the year. It appears that he did not see fit to advise his board that his 'ultimate aim', as we saw earlier, was to place Justine with a white family. The board accepted his recommendation.

Unaware that the board had already met, Mrs Sampson submitted to them a three-page letter outlining her complaint:

> I am the mother of my girl & I want her here with me, & no person has the right to refuse me that privilege. I want you good people to Realise that no one can care for my Daughter & give her the same Care as I her mother can.[36]

On then being told that Justine would remain at Koonibba until the end of the year, Mrs Sampson again wrote to Penhall:

> This board, Sir, of which you is secretary is trying to bring into operation something that was never intended by His Majesty Parliament. Namely to break that Mother Love of which we hold dear and to separate one from that which [is] sacred to us. I trust that the board will reconsider their harsh decision and give my application a more humane consideration.[37]

It didn't. In fact it appears that this letter was not even presented to the board.

In May 1940, Carol Wilkinson, of Yantanabie, requested of Penhall that her sister Lorna be allowed to have a holiday with her. Traeger had told her that the Koonibba Mission Board was against the proposal. Lorna, being held against her will in the Koonibba Children's Home, was soon to turn 30! Carol wrote: 'my poor sister dreads to think, she's to spend all her days in the Mission Home.'[38]

A month later, Penhall advised Mrs Wilkinson that Traeger had 'authorised' Lorna to spend one month with her.[39] Of course, neither Traeger nor Penhall had any such authority over Lorna's movements.

The keeping of Aboriginal women in the Koonibba Children's Home after they had turned 18 was to become known, rather inaccurately, as the '21 rule'. This 'rule' stipulated that young Aboriginal women should not be allowed out of the home until the age of 21, unless to marry. But, as indicated above, some were kept way past their 21st birthday. As long as they remained in the home, they continued to be a source of very cheap labour. An official Koonibba Mission document notes: 'The older girls are taught to assist the matrons with the cooking, cleaning, sewing, washing, ironing and mending – an almost endless task when there are about fifty children to care for ...'[40]

By July 1940, Mrs Sampson had engaged a solicitor to help her in the return of her daughter Justine. She was to find that Penhall could even take her right to legal representation from her. When her lawyer called on Penhall to discuss the release of Justine, Penhall convinced him not to continue with the case. According to Penhall: 'He [the lawyer] agreed that the child is best off at Koonibba.'[41]

Three months later, Traeger requested that arrangements be made for Justine to be sent to Victoria to work for Lutherans.[42] Penhall advised Traeger to wait until the end of the year, when his board would review her case.[43]

By December 1940, Pastor Hoff's aim was to place Justine in 'a suitable white home'[44] in Adelaide. Penhall agreed and made a recommendation to his board to allow this,[45] but stipulated to Traeger that she be found a situation close to Koonibba. He feared that if she were placed in or near Adelaide she would make contact with the Point Pearce community.[46] This brings into question the accuracy of her reported reluctance to have contact with her people, notably her mother.

In January 1941, Traeger arranged for Justine, now aged 14, to be sent to work for a Mr Alec Thomson, of Talia.[47] Her mother was not told.

In the same month, the '21 rule' again became an issue at Koonibba, with Deborah Doyle writing to Penhall to advise him that, though she was over 21 years of age, Traeger had told her that she needed Penhall's permission in order to return to her sick mother at Coorabie, to help her.[48] Of course, she did not need this permission.

When asked by Penhall to explain the situation, Traeger argued that, though Deborah's mother was ill, she had been ill for a long time and would be sent to hospital if she became worse. This being the case, he argued, there was no need for Deborah to go to her, and she should only be allowed to leave the Koonibba Home if she could get work as a domestic on a station: '[Deborah]'s chief concern seems to be to get out of the Children's Home.'[49]

Penhall duly advised Deborah to try to obtain work at a station near her mother, and, from there, occasionally visit her.[50] He could not, he told her, give her permission to live with her mother.[51] It was a permission he had no authority to withhold. His action here was entirely unsupported by law, and in fact he had both a legal and a moral duty to inform Deborah that she was free to do as she wished.

The issue surfaced again in July 1941. After discussing the matter with the Koonibba Mission Board[52], Penhall advised Traeger to train children in the home until they were 18 and then 'send them out to service'.[53] The following day, Penhall made this same recommendation to his board.[54] The recommendation was approved. This should have been the end of the '21 rule'.

Six months later, Marielena Kennedy, an inmate of the Koonibba Children's Home, requested permission to go to her mother for a month. In her letter to Traeger she indicated she would turn 21 in February. Traeger informed Penhall:

> This request could be granted. [Marielana] should be told that she must return to Koonibba at the end of her stay at Lock. Her reference to being 21, may possibly also be an indication that she does not wish to return to Koonibba Children's Home. It would be in her own interests to return as her parents live very primitively.[55]

Penhall then wrote to Kennedy, perpetuating the deception that she was not free to leave the home permanently: 'I am agreeable to you paying a visit to your mother on condition that at the end of one month you return to the home at Koonibba.'[56] In doing this, he was disregarding his own board's ruling on the matter.

The structures of authority set up by Traeger and Penhall, and especially the requirement that Aboriginal people repeatedly be required to make written applications, were clearly designed to crush any sense of independence among the Aboriginal residents of Koonibba. Most of the correspondence Penhall received from the inmates of the mission was sent back to Traeger for his information and comment. For Traeger, the benefits of this arrangement were obvious. Not only did he know the identity of those Aboriginal people who dared complain about his administration, the procedure itself would have had the effect of reducing the number of their complaints. They were well aware that all of their complaints were returned to Traeger.

In this regime, children as young as five years old could be made prisoners of the Koonibba Children's Home. In July 1942, Mrs Joyce Webb informed Penhall that her only child, her five-year-old daughter, was an inmate of the home. In a familiar pattern, obviously designed to wear down dissenting Aboriginal parents, Traeger had asked Mrs Webb to write to Penhall for permission for her release. Her letter ends: 'Shes only small girl. I am lonely without her, shes in the home.'[57] When asked to comment on this case, Traeger gave several reasons for refusing her request including that she had separated from her husband.[58] Penhall duly informed Mrs Webb that her request could not be considered.[59]

Young Aboriginal women and school-aged children were the twin targets of Traeger's program of enforced residency. Towards the end of 1943, he wrote to Penhall regarding the Shaws. Over the past few years, they had become increasingly reluctant to return their children to Koonibba after school holidays, and police officers at Iron Knob and Wudinna 'were kept busy for quite a time' returning them the previous year.[60] Traeger decided to detain their children in the home for the holidays that year, and also the children of several other families.[61]

Penhall fell into line with Traeger's plan. He sent letters to the Shaws and another family, notifying them that their children were to stay at Koonibba over the Christmas break.[62] Traeger was to decide which children were allowed to go on holidays with their parents.[63]

Discontent among the Aboriginal residents of Koonibba was evident in February 1944, when welfare officer McKenzie visited the mission. She reported that conditions at Koonibba were far from ideal: there was unhappiness among parents with the staffing of the children's home, and people were drifting away 'as they don't like sharing [their] homes [with other families] and they like their children to attend school with white children'. She continued, 'Only one [Aboriginal] man ... is employed on Koonibba so the men must go away to work and like to take their families with them.'[64]

It may also be that Aboriginal parents, aware that the department was not prepared to rein in Traeger's increasing megalomania, were reacting by removing their children from his reach. Towards the end of 1944, Traeger reported that 16 children, including 14 from the home, had not returned to school following holidays in Ceduna with their parents. He fumed: 'None of these people should leave Koonibba with their children unless they arrange for return in time for school.'[65]

Penhall obliged by writing to three of the mothers involved, advising them that they were to leave their children in the home even during school holidays – and so permanently. He had no legal authority to do this. Even if there was cause for such directives, they were matters for his board.

In March 1944, the case of Mrs Sampson and her daughter Justine re-emerged. Mrs Sampson asked if Justine was still at Kondulka Station.[66] Penhall requested information from Traeger, who replied: 'She is still at Kondulka as far as I know. At Christmas time she was engaged to [Arthur Daniels], of Pt. Lincoln, a very desirable young man (half-caste).'[67]

Penhall's letter to the manager of Point Pearce Station, for the information of Mrs Sampson, was deliberately brief. The message reads in its entirety: 'Please advise Mrs. [Damien Sampson] that her daughter, [Justine Reynolds], is still at Kondulka Station and is quite well.'[68] There was no mention of her impending marriage. It was now six years since Mrs Sampson's initial attempt to have her daughter returned.

Throughout 1944, Terry Mason made several attempts to get his daughter, Rachel, released from the Koonibba Home. Being over 18, she was 'employed' in the home, which, as we have seen, was a euphemism for being held there under the '21 rule'. Mrs Taylor, of Streaky Bay, was prepared to employ her, and wrote to Penhall on this subject several times at Mr Mason's request.[69] Traeger's response is typically dismissive of the rights of Aboriginal parents, and hints at the dictatorial and oppressive regime he created at Koonibba:

> [Terry Mason]'s wish and opinion does not count for very much. He is a father rich in daughters which a kindly institution has reared for him ... When he speaks to me, and I tell him his girl is needed in the Home and that her first duty is there as we have brought up all his girls, he agrees with a smile.[70]

In regard to this oppressive atmosphere, the following paragraph from an official Koonibba publication is illuminating:

> One would need to write a book to explain why the government of a mission station is so intricate and difficult. Suffice it to say that most natives are still under tutelage (*unmuendig*). Therefore the man who acts as superintendent has duties towards them similar in many ways to those of a father of a family of under-age children. Multiply the average family by about two hundred and you have the problem.[71]

Rachel was still in the home in November 1944, when Mrs Taylor approached Premier Playford directly in order to obtain her services.[72] Penhall again supported the regime at Koonibba, advising his minister that Rachel's services were required at Koonibba but that Mrs Taylor could have her choice of either Rosslyn Gordon or Sarah Clark, also residents of Koonibba Mission.[73]

The Lutherans were clearly interested in the income-generating aspect of institutionalising Aboriginal children, a practice which had its counterpart in the pastoral industry, where it was known as 'nigger farming'. Traeger controlled the Commonwealth child endowment payments for all of the children in the Home.

By June 1944, there were 46 children in the Koonibba Home.[74] When Traeger found out that three large Aboriginal families were leaving Koonibba, he attempted to disrupt their plans. He wrote a feverish letter to the Deputy Commissioner of Child Endowment, arguing that the three families 'should get their endowment only at Koonibba, where a large school has been built for these children'.[75]

Two of the families Traeger was most concerned about were the Bakers and, as we have seen, the Shaws. Both had settled in the town of Wudinna. Traeger withheld their child endowment while he waited for a ruling from the deputy commissioner on whether they should be allowed to receive it away from the mission.[76] In the meantime, welfare officer McKenzie visited Wudinna and reported that Mary Baker's house and children were dirty and she could not pay her rent because her child endowment was not being sent on from Koonibba: 'When asked why she has not had her money transferred she replied that she thought she would return to Koonibba as she couldn't make a do of it!'[77]

The Aborigines Department was well aware that Traeger was withholding her money illegally. Instead of requesting Traeger to send it on, Penhall asked the Wudinna police to bring pressure upon Mary Baker to return with her family to the mission.[78]

Traeger was also concerned about the possibility of losing the child endowment brought into the mission by the Lawson family. It was Matthew Lawson, who, as we saw earlier, spoke out against the forced indenture of Koonibba children to Lutheran families in 1936. This had obviously not endeared him to the mission authorities.

In mid 1944, while Traeger was receiving medical treatment at the Ceduna Hospital, Matthew Lawson left Koonibba Mission[79] for the small town of Minnipa with his wife, Christine, and their children. Such was the oppressive regime at Koonibba that it appears that the Lawsons saw Traeger's hospitalisation as their chance to leave.

Within days of Traeger informing Penhall of the Lawsons' departure, McKenzie visited them at Minnipa. She reported that they were living in 'an empty unlined iron house' with no furniture. Lawson was not working and Traeger was withholding their child endowment. They had no money and were in debt: 'The children are not going to school and [Christine] is very unhappy.'[80]

Penhall requested of the Minnipa police that Matthew Lawson be told to return his family to Koonibba immediately.[81] To Traeger he wrote: 'unless [Lawson] is prepared to work and save for these children in a proper manner, it will be necessary to take action to remove them from his control.'[82] This threat appears to have been relayed to the Lawsons. They returned to Koonibba almost immediately, with Traeger writing to Penhall: 'Thank you for your prompt action.'[83]

The following month, Judy Lawson, Matthew's daughter, asked Penhall for permission to visit her parents on the mission each day. They were now both unwell; Judy was an inmate of the home. Traeger had told her father to apply to Penhall for permission.[84] When asked to comment on this seemingly reasonable request, Traeger typically argued that Judy should stay in the home and not be allowed to visit her parents.[85] Penhall, typically, fell in line and refused Judy's request.

Matthew Lawson, however, was not to be outdone by Traeger and Penhall. He persisted in his attempts to have Judy released from the home, and it is here that we have further evidence of Traeger's manipulations and Penhall's tendency to ignore them. In late August 1944, Traeger told Penhall that he had interviewed the Lawsons regarding Judy, 'and they state that they do not want her'.[86]

At the same time, however, and again two weeks later, Lawson wrote to Penhall, reiterating that he wanted Judy released from the home and into his custody, and complaining that he was still to receive a satisfactory answer from Penhall to his earlier correspondence on the matter.[87] Asked by Penhall to explain this discrepancy, Traeger noted: 'He admits that he told me one thing and wrote something else to you. He stated that he would write you saying that he was sorry he wrote about this matter.'[88]

Still Penhall did not deign to reply to Lawson, who by mid October was frustrated and disenchanted enough to write a long letter with the following, sarcastic ending: 'I got no answer from you of that letter, but all the same I [k] now where that letter return. I am blind. I no [sic] nothing. Yours truly, [M. Lawson].'[89]

In January 1945, Lawson told Penhall that he would not return Judy to the Home following her end of year holiday. At this point, Traeger appears to have given up on the idea of illegally holding Judy, advising Penhall that he thought it best for Lawson to care for his own daughter.[90] Within months, however, Traeger had been instrumental in having Lawson's 14-year-old son committed to the Magill Reformatory, to remain there until the age of 18.

Matthew and Christine Lawson maintained that their son was innocent of the offence he had been charged with, and an eyewitness account told of his 'confession' being beaten out of him by Traeger and Lange, the head teacher at Koonibba. In July 1945, the Lawsons again left the mission, settling in the town of Lock. Traeger, monomaniacally intent on crushing the Lawsons and their protest, again insisted that they be returned to him: 'If [Lawsons] get away with this move, we will have all the larger families over hill and dale. They are talking very strongly about that now.'[91]

The Lawsons, as far as Traeger was concerned, were to be used to make an example of his power and authority, as the loss of 'larger families' certainly meant the loss of mission income. McKenzie visited the Lawsons in August 1945:

> Visited Mrs [Fred Bennett] & Mrs [Matt Lawson] living in a house a mile out of the town. They seem quite happy & contented, and have no wish to return to Koonibba. Mrs [Lawson] would like me to visit [Justin] at Magill. The children seem to be fitting in quite well at Lock school & the teacher has no complaints as to their behaviour & cleanliness.[92]

Penhall relayed this information to Traeger and, with rare consideration for the rights of an Aboriginal family of Koonibba, recommended that 'so long as they are living under the circumstances outlined above, no action [should] be taken to send them back to Koonibba'.[93] Traeger exacted a small measure of revenge the next winter when he refused Lawson's request for ration blankets for his family.[94]

In May 1946, the Koonibba board appointed a lay superintendent to run the mission, with Traeger to remain as missionary and solely in charge of 'spiritual' matters.[95] Traeger resigned from his work at Koonibba six months later and moved to Broken Hill. He thanked Penhall for his 'kindly and considerate manner in your many dealings with me'.[96] Penhall responded in kind: 'I note your kindly remarks regarding our mutual association, and I desire to thank you most sincerely for the help you have given during your stay at Koonibba.'[97]

The new superintendent, C.V. Eckermann, had served as an assistant to Traeger five years previously.[98] Eckermann continued the Koonibba tradition of illegally holding Aboriginal children against the wishes of their parents, a tradition which continued to be supported by the Aborigines Department. On 27 December 1946, he telegrammed the department: 'In view of number of immoralities during past period I want to keep all girls over [the age of] ten in home over Xmas holidays. Parents objecting strenuously. Have I the authority as Superintendent to keep them.'[99] Bray, the acting secretary of the department in the absence of Penhall, told him he did. This was a lie.

Eckermann did, however, recognise that people such as Matthew Lawson and his family deserved better than what Koonibba could offer. By 1948, Lawson was at Yeelanna, working on the Trans Australian railway line, and had applied for an exemption from the Act. Eckermann noted that Lawson had been 'a steady worker and has maintained his family well': 'His home at Maltee, whenever I saw it, was a credit to him; although it would be more accurate to say that the credit was due to his wife, who is an excellent housekeeper.'[100]

While not recommending he be exempted, more praise was to follow. In May 1948, Eckermann praised Lawson and backed his plea for the release of his son from the reformatory: 'He has cared well for his children.'[101] In this same month, the board gave Lawson and his family limited exemption from the Act.[102]

Eckermann also had a different approach to the '21 rule', or the 'older girls rule' as he called it. The Sinclair and Knight families had refused to send their younger children back to the home, as a protest against the rule that older girls were not to be released for holidays. Eckermann wanted to retain the 'older girls rule', which he described as 'the last remnant of a salutary protective control which Koonibba used to be able to exercise over the welfare of the young native girls', but would reluctantly drop it if it was the only means of getting the children back.[103] In fairness to Eckermann, he appears to have been genuinely concerned that the children were not receiving an education.

However, over the following months he appears to have hardened his stance. Following strong urging from the Koonibba Mission and local police, Penhall recommended to his board that children were to be released from the Koonibba Children's Home only with the board's permission:

> A number of natives, including [Sinclair] and [Knight], have prevailed upon the officials of the Mission to allow the children to leave the Home during the Christmas vacation, which is spent in the camps occupied by the parents, and then, when the date agreed upon for the return of the children comes, the parents leave the district taking their children with them.
>
> It would appear that the time has arrived when the Board must take strong measures to protect the children against the indolence and vices of their parents.[104]

The board approved this recommendation. Eckermann, however, was reasonable enough to reconsider his position in the face of its patent unfairness. He advised Penhall:

> [Bradley Knight]'s children have been placed in the Home. [Knight] and his wife have taken the matter as a sore blow, and are nothing short of heart broken over the fact that their child, [Dorothy], aged six, is also in the Home. [Knight]'s wife literally has wept incessantly for the past two days over this. They do not mind the older children being in the home, and are willing to allow [Dorothy]'s admission when she is a few years older, but ask that they be allowed to send [Dorothy] to school from a home on the station. We strongly recommend that this request be granted ...[105]

Traeger was incapable of writing a letter like this. Penhall immediately endorsed this arrangement, apparently without communicating the change to his board. Penhall, of course, had no authority to alter a recommendation of the board. It is highly likely that to reveal the full story to the board, with Eckermann's description of the traumatic consequences of removing children from Aboriginal parents, might have encouraged the 'unpractical' members of the board to question the usefulness and fairness of such actions generally.[106]

Eckermann, to his credit, continued to have misgivings about the '21 rule'. In mid 1952, under very acrimonious circumstances, Harrie Green resigned as superintendent of the Ooldea Mission. The Koonibba authorities were instructed by the department to remove the Ooldea people to Colona Station, some 130 kilometres due south of Ooldea. Eckermann sought advice from Penhall on the policy of keeping Ooldean children in the Koonibba Home. Faced with extreme reluctance on the part of the Ooldeans to part with their daughters given the '21 rule', Eckermann again broached the possibility of its demise. He confided that he had 'long felt misgivings regarding the policy', considering the 'sanctity' of 'family ties, parental rights, and the natural affection between parent and child'.[107]

Penhall missed this opportunity to ensure that Aboriginal parents at Koonibba were treated with respect and in accordance with their legal rights. He merely recommended a conference on the issue – a conference which was never to occur – and suggested the matter 'remain in abeyance' unless specifically challenged by the parents of the Ooldea children.

Penhall's reluctance to change the Koonibba regime is symptomatic of his general reluctance to provide the Aboriginal residents of Koonibba Mission with information about their legal rights, and especially their rights as parents. Worse than this omission, however, the directives that Penhall gave Koonibba residents in relation to the custody of their children were generally without legal authority.

It is appropriate that Mrs King, who, as we saw earlier, lost several daughters to the Koonibba Children's Home, should have the last word:

> All these years I live here, there is no Christian Love shown amongst the White people here. There is enough proof will be published one of these days, & I hope my words will come true.[108]

CHAPTER SEVEN

'Legally indefensible', concluding remarks

'UNDER THE ABORIGINES ACT, THE BOARD HAS NO POWER WHATEVER TO REMOVE CHILDREN FROM THEIR PARENTS.'

PENHALL TO FRANCIS BARNES, 30 NOVEMBER 1951, GRG 52/1/1951/49

Geoffrey Bolton, the distinguished historian, has warned against disparaging those individuals who administered policies which we regard today with disdain. Bolton suggests that 'when policies become unpopular in the passing of time, the verdict of history has sometimes blamed the bureaucrat rather than the politicians or the community whom both served'.[1]

Generally speaking, this is good advice. During the mid twentieth century the South Australian Government proved itself remarkably unsympathetic to Aboriginal issues, leading to an environment in which Aboriginal children could be removed or withheld from their parents without regard for legal process.

While, at first blush perhaps, it appears that the board *could* confine Aboriginal children to, for example, the Colebrook Home or Umeewarra Mission under sections 10 and 17 of the Act, it was section 38 which applied to the removal of Aboriginal children from their parents:

> (1) The [Aborigines Protection] board may, with the approval of the Children's Welfare and Public Relief Board ... commit any aboriginal child to any institution within the meaning of the Maintenance Act, 1926, under the control of the Children's Welfare and Public Relief Board, to be there detained or otherwise dealt with under the said Act until such child attains the age of eighteen years.

This makes the South Australian legislation different from that which operated in Western Australia, Queensland and the Northern Territory, none of which had legislative regimes which allowed the direct transfer of guardianship of an Aboriginal child from its protectors or boards to their mainstream welfare departments. This point appears to have been overlooked by those who have written on the subject of Aboriginal guardianship. They have tended to assume that the circumstances of Aboriginal guardianship in South Australia did not differ from that which held in the other states. Further, within the South Australian legislation, there was no explicit mention of the capacity to remove a child from its parents, as found for instance in section 18 of the corresponding Queensland Act. Given this, Aboriginal guardianship in South Australia may have been of a weaker kind than that which normally operates.[2]

Using sections 10 and 17 of the South Australian Act to effect *the removal of a child from its parents* was clearly outside the spirit of the legislation. In any case, two points should be kept in mind. Firstly, it was *the board*, not Penhall himself, which had the power to act; secondly, in many of the cases we have examined there appears not to have been any formal invocation of section 17 of the Act, and no corresponding paperwork to support the removal of children.

Indeed section 17 appears to have been rarely invoked. It was used in December 1924, when Chief Protector Garnett requested that police be instructed to return a 14-year-old girl to the Koonibba Mission under this part of the Act.[3] And then, in late 1925, two Aboriginal girls were served with notices to return to Point Pearce under the same section. At the time, Garnett advised the superintendent of the station to keep the copies of the notices 'as you will need them if legal action should be necessary'.[4] Again, at Koonibba in 1930, an Aboriginal man who complained of his harsh treatment at the hands of the authorities there, and the whipping of others, was compelled to return to the mission under section 17 of the Act. A notice to this effect was given to him by a police officer.[5]

It appears then that a written notice to use section 17 was an essential element of its use. However, throughout the 1940s, when children were removed or withheld from their parents by the board, there is no evidence of written notices being issued.

Although under section 10 of the Act the board was the legal guardian of all Aboriginal children under the age of 21, it appears there were just two ways that they could legally cause an Aboriginal child to be committed to an institution against the wishes of the child's parents. Firstly, they could use section 38 to effect a direct 'transfer of control' of a child from their guardianship to that of the

CWPRB. Secondly, they could refer a case to the CWPRB in order that it use its general procedure – as used for the white population – to commit a child.

Towards the end of 1951, Penhall received several letters from Francis Barnes, of Alice Springs, who was attempting to have his daughter removed from her Aboriginal mother. Penhall advised Barnes:

> In a previous similar case, I obtained an opinion from the Crown Solicitor regarding the power of the Board, and was informed that, under the Aborigines Act, *the Board has no power whatever to remove children from their parents.* For this reason it will be seen that I have to proceed very carefully, as I do not wish to be obliged to defend an action which is legally indefensible.
>
> On the general question of removing children, I have been advised that the only way in which this can be done is to notify the Children's Welfare Department if any child is believed to be ill treated or neglected, and that Department makes enquiries and institutes any proceedings the Head of the Department may consider necessary [emphasis added].[6]

This demonstrates clearly that Penhall had been advised by the Crown Solicitor that his board was not permitted to remove Aboriginal children from their parents. In 2007, in the landmark Stolen Generation test case brought by Bruce Trevorrow against the South Australian Government, the Hon. Justice Gray found that Penhall advised his board, in August 1949:

> The Crown Solicitor has advised that the [APB] has no authority to remove aboriginal children from their parents except by concerted action with the [CWPRB], as provided in section 38 of the Aborigines Act, 1934–39.[7]

Why did Penhall remove or withhold Aboriginal children from their parents? The answer lies at least in part in his Christian world view. In August 1944, Penhall agreed with Inspector Bourke, of the Port Augusta police, that a mission was needed near Oodnadatta. As an occasional lay preacher, Penhall believed that Christian missionary involvement was to the benefit of Aboriginal children:

> The children rescued from camp life and placed in institutions respond remarkably well to kindness, good food, and general supervision by Christian Missionaries, and it seems to me that this method of dealing with the aboriginal race offers the best prospect of success. So long as the children continue to grow up in the old environment, there cannot be any radical change in the character of the people.[8]

It is entirely possible that he believed, in most of the cases we have seen, that he was 'doing the right thing'. However, it is clear that Penhall failed to come to a sympathetic, intelligent understanding of Aboriginal people and their complicated plight in the context of colonial history. This failure of imagination, intellect and feeling allowed him to act as if his Aboriginal charges were themselves responsible for their own condition. The negativity towards them that he cultivated and encouraged allowed him to disregard *their* wishes, hopes and dreams, and to consider them as something lesser than the general, white population.

The world-renowned Australian anthropologists, Ronald and Catherine Berndt, had several dealings with Penhall in the mid 1940s. They blamed him for the death of an elderly man who had tirelessly and patiently helped them with their anthropological research. At the age of 78 he was evicted from his home, despite his appeals for clemency, and despite Penhall having promised the Berndts that he would not be evicted. He died soon after. The Berndts wrote, almost 50 years after the event: 'As we write this, our anger at this callous act is undiminished.'[9] Of Penhall, they wrote: 'The reputation among Aboriginal people of this official Protector of Aborigines was perhaps the worst among all of those we have known.'[10]

In line with his practice of not drawing attention to himself or his department, there appears to be no photograph of Penhall either in the government archives or in the 14,000-strong glass negative collection held by the History Trust of South Australia. There is, however, a photograph of Penhall in a published pamphlet.[11] Taken at the unveiling of a memorial for Reverend George Taplin at Point McLeay on 23 July 1950, it shows Reverend Gordon Rowe, David Unaipon, Malcolm McIntosh (MP), Professor Cleland, Penhall and others.

We can agree generally with Bolton's comments regarding bureaucrats and blame. Penhall cannot be blamed for the paucity of funds made available to him, nor perhaps even for some aspects of the general mismanagement of Aboriginal affairs during his time as the head of the Aborigines Department. However, the story of Penhall's administration consists of a litany of acts of commission and omission that point to his failure to bring an intelligent and sympathetic reading to Aboriginal affairs. He failed grossly to come to an understanding of the Aboriginal situation.

In the photograph, Penhall, clearly the tallest of the men present, is standing a step or two back from the group, who form a semicircle in front of the monument. Head bowed, it is as if he doesn't want to have his photograph taken, or be there at all.

APPENDIX

THE ABORIGINES ACT 1934–1939

Section 7 (the duties of the board)

7. It shall be the duty of the board—
   (a) to apportion, distribute, and apply, as seems most fit, the moneys at the disposal of the board:
   (b) in its discretion, to apply part of the moneys at its disposal in the purchase of stock and implements to be loaned to aborigines to whom land has been allotted under section 18, and may supply the same accordingly either without payment or on such terms as are approved by the board, and no person shall, except with the approval of the board, acquire any title to any goods or chattels so loaned as aforesaid:
   (c) to distribute blankets, clothing, provisions, and other relief or assistance to the aborigines:
   (d) to provide, as far as practicable, for the supply of food, medical attendance, medicines, and shelter for the sick, aged, and infirm aborigines:
   (e) to provide, when possible, for the custody, maintenance and education of the children of the aborigines:

(f) to manage and regulate the use of all reserves for aborigines:
(g) to exercise a general supervision and care over all matters affecting the welfare of the aborigines, and to protect them against injustice, imposition, and fraud.

Section 10 (1) (legal guardianship of Aboriginal children)
The board shall be the legal guardian of every aboriginal child, notwithstanding that any such child has a parent or other relative living, until such child attains the age of twenty-one years, except whilst such child is a State child within the meaning of the Maintenance Act, 1926.

Section 17 (1) (the power to remove Aboriginal people to reserves)
The board may cause any aborigine to be kept within the boundaries of any reserve or aboriginal institution, or to be removed to and kept within the boundaries of any reserve or aboriginal institution, or to be removed from one reserve or aboriginal institution to another reserve or aboriginal institution, and to be kept therein.

Section 38 (1) (the transfer of control of an Aboriginal child to the CWPRB)
The board may, with the approval of the Children's Welfare and Public Relief Board constituted under the Maintenance Act, 1926, commit any aboriginal child to any institution within the meaning of the Maintenance Act, 1926, under the control of the Children's Welfare and Public Relief Board, to be there detained or otherwise dealt with under the said Act until such child attains the age of eighteen years.

Section 39 (1) (the effect of transfer of control)
Upon the execution of the said transfer of control with respect to any aboriginal child, such child shall become a State child within the meaning of the Maintenance Act, 1926, and all the provisions of the said Act shall apply to and in respect of such child as if such child were a neglected child ...

THE ABORIGINES (TRAINING OF CHILDREN) ACT 1923

Sections 6 and 7 (the transfer of control of an Aboriginal child to the State Children's Council)

6. (1) The Chief Protector may, with the approval of the State Children's Council constituted under the State Children Act, 1895, commit any aboriginal child to any institution within the meaning of the State Children Act, 1895, under the control of the said Council, to be there detained or otherwise dealt with under the said Act until such child attains the age of eighteen years.
(2) Such approval and commitment shall be in writing in the form of the Transfer of Control contained in the Schedule to this Act, or in a form to the like effect.
7. (1) Upon the execution of the said Transfer of Control with respect to any aboriginal child, such child shall become a State child within the meaning of the State Children Act, 1895, and all the provisions of the said Act shall apply to and in respect of such child as if such child were a neglected child committed under the said Act to the institution specified in the said Transfer, and as if the said Transfer were the mandate issued under the said Act for the taking of such child to such institution and for the detention of such child until such child attains the age of eighteen years, subject to the said Act.

NOTES

PREFACE

1 Elkin, A.P. 1979, 'Aboriginal-European relations in Western Australia: an historical and personal record', in R.M. and C.H. Berndt (eds) *Aborigines of the west: their past and their present*, University of Western Australia Press, Perth, p. 299.

CHAPTER 1

The blacks' camp, 1911–1920

1 See GRG 52/1/1911/21.
2 Mounted Constable W. Ahern, 10 August 1911, GRG 52/1/1911/21.
3 South Australia, Parliament 1911, Annual Report of Aborigines Department, 16 September 1911, GRG 52/1/1911/29.
4 R.J. Matheson, Manager, Nilpena Station, to Inspector Clode, 13 September 1911, GRG 52/1/1911/30.
5 South to Matheson, 20 September 1911, GRG 52/1/1911/30.
6 South Australia, Parliament 1911, Parliamentary Paper no. 30, 1911.
7 Section 10 of the Aborigines Act.
8 Section 17 of the Aborigines Act.
9 South Australia, House of Assembly 1911, Debates, vol. 1, p. 417.
10 State Children's Department, Report on Congress, 20 June 1911, GRG 52/1/1911/_.

11 GRG 52/1/1910/2.
12 State Children's Department, Report on Congress, 20 June 1911, GRG 52/1/1911/_.
13 State Children's Department, Report on Congress, 20 June 1911, GRG 52/1/1911/_.
14 South to Commissioner of Public Works, 13 May 1913, GRG 52/1/1913/18.
15 Mounted Constable Redpath to Sub-Inspector Rumball, Mt Gambier, 12 June 1913, GRG 52/1/1913/18.
16 Gray, Secretary, State Children's Council, 1 July 1913, GRG 52/1/1913/18.
17 Senior Constable Morris, Bordertown, to Inspector Rumball, 21 July 1913, GRG 52/1/1913/18.
18 South Australia, Parliament 1914, Report of the State Children's Council for the year ended 30 June 1914, Parliamentary Paper no. 20.
19 South Australia, Parliament 1915, Annual Report of the State Children's Council for the year ended 30 June 1915, Parliamentary Paper no. 20.
20 South Australia, Parliament 1917, Government Gazette, 10 May 1917, pp. 742–743.
21 South Australia, Parliament 1919, Government Gazette, 21 August 1919, p. 383.

CHAPTER 2

In the hands of one man, 1921–1938

1 South Australia, House of Assembly 1921, Debates, vol. 2, pp. 1466–1467.
2 South Australia, House of Assembly 1921, Debates, vol. 2, p. 1573.
3 South Australia, House of Assembly 1921, Debates, vol. 2, p. 1576.
4 Sections 6 and 7(i) of the Aborigines Act.
5 South Australia, Legislative Council 1923, Debates, vol. 2, p. 1015.
6 South Australia, House of Assembly 1923, Debates, vol. 1, p. 738.
7 Chief Protector to Superintendent, Point McLeay, 10 January 1924, GRG 52/1/1924/2.
8 Chief Protector Garnett to Secretary, State Children's Council, 25 March 1924, GRG 52/1/1924/21.
9 Rev. Sexton to Chief Protector, 2 May 1924, GRG 52/1/1924/14.
10 Garnett to Commissioner of Public Works, 2 May 1924, GRG 52/1/1924/21.
11 I have been reliably informed that there is advice of this sort from the Crown Solicitor to the Aborigines Department, circa 1961. I know the number of the file in which this advice is contained. However, I have been refused permission by the Attorney-General to view the file in question.
12 South Australia, Parliament 1918, Government Gazette, 24 January 1918, p. 141.
13 See GRG 52/1/1925/18.
14 South Australia, Parliament 1925, Government Gazette, 7 May 1925, p. 839.
15 McLean to Commissioner of Public Works, 4 November 1932, GRG 52/1/1930/42.
16 GRG 52/1/1926/37.
17 Harvey and Sexton to ACA, 1 November 1926 and forwarded to Commissioner of Public Works, GRG 52/1/1926/62.
18 GRG 52/1/1926/62.
19 Dickey, B. 1986, *Rations, residence, resources: a history of social welfare in South Australia since 1836*, Wakefield Press, Adelaide, p. 180.
20 South Australia, House of Assembly 1927, Debates, vol. 2, p. 1858.
21 W.H. Harvey, Chairman, ACA, to Chief Protector, 4 June 1930, GRG 52/1/1930/28.

22 Garnett to Commissioner of Public Works, 5 June 1930, GRG 52/1/1930/28.
23 Commissioner of Public Works to Chief Protector, 10 June 1930, GRG 52/1/1930/28.
24 South Australia, Parliament 1930, Government Gazette, 9 October 1930, p. 754.
25 South Australia, Parliament 1930, Government Gazette, 25 December 1930, p. 1295.
26 GRG 52/1/1930/65.
27 GRG 52/1/1930/65, p. 7.
28 Acting Chief Protector McLean to Penhall, 10 January 1931, GRG 52/1/1930/65.
29 Gibbs, R.M. 1984, *A history of South Australia: from colonial days to the present*, Southern Heritage, Blackwood, Adelaide, p. 201.
30 South Australia, Parliament 1931, Government Gazette, 19 February 1931, p. 311.
31 South Australia, Parliament 1933, Government Gazette, 9 March 1933, p. 372.
32 South Australia, House of Assembly 1936, Debates, 10 November 1936, p. 2293.
33 McLean to Chairman, Children's Welfare Department, 18 July 1933, GRG 52/1/1933/17.
34 Chairman, Children's Welfare and Public Relief Board, to Under Secretary, 4 August 1933, GRG 52/1/1933/17.
35 Chairman, Children's Welfare and Public Relief Board, to Under Secretary, 19 February 1930, GRG 52/1/1930/5.
36 GRG 52/1/1934/41.
37 Penhall to Superintendent, Koonibba Mission, 29 October 1934, GRG 52/1/1934/29.
38 GRG 52/1/1934/50.
39 South Australia, House of Assembly 1934, Debates, p. 1492.
40 South Australia, House of Assembly 1936, Debates, 12 November 1936, p. 2419.
41 South Australia, House of Assembly 1936, Debates, 30 June 1936, vol. 1, p. 358.
42 South Australia, House of Assembly 1936, Debates, vol. 2, p. 2424.
43 South Australia, House of Assembly 1936, Debates, vol. 2, p. 2425.
44 South Australia, Legislative Council 1936, Debates, vol. 2, p. 2588.
45 South Australia, House of Assembly 1934, Debates, p. 2236.
46 Aiston to Chief Protector, 5 August 1937, GRG 52/1/1937/48.
47 South Australia, Parliament 1911, Annual Report of State Children's Council, Parliamentary Paper no. 20.
48 For a discussion of whether the 'absorptionist' programs of the Northern Territory, Western Australia and South Australia in the 1920s and 1930s could be considered genocidal, see Manne, R. 2004, 'Aboriginal child removal and the question of genocide, 1900–1940' in D. Moses (ed.) *Genocide and settler society: frontier violence and stolen Indigenous children in Australian history*, Berghahn Books, New York.
49 Penhall to Public Service Commissioner, 27 September 1938, GRG 52/1/1934/50.
50 South Australia, Parliament 1938, Government Gazette, 6 October 1938, p. 920.
51 South Australia, Parliament 1938, Government Gazette, 10 November 1938, p. 1231.
52 Penhall to Commissioner of Public Works, 15 September 1938, GRG 52/1/1936/55.
53 Penhall to Commissioner of Public Works, 15 September 1938, GRG 52/1/1936/55.

CHAPTER THREE

This practice has no regulation to support it, 1939–1946

1 South Australia, House of Assembly 1939, Debates, vol. 1, p. 882.

2 Cockburn, S. 1991, *Playford: Benevolent Despot*, Axiom Publishers, Kent Town, South Australia, p. viii.
3 Howell, P.A. 1996, 'Playford, politics and parliament', in *Playford's South Australia: essays on the history of South Australia 1933–1968*, Association of Professional Historians Inc, Adelaide, p. 56.
4 Cockburn, 1991, p. 193.
5 *Advertiser*, 29 January 1940, p. 8.
6 South Australia, Parliament 1940, Government Gazette, 25 January 1940, p. 117.
7 South Australia, Parliament 1940, Government Gazette, 25 January 1940, p. 119.
8 South Australia, Parliament 1940, Government Gazette, 1 February 1940, p. 171.
9 See Buti, A.D. 2004, *Separated: Aboriginal childhood separations and guardianship law*, Sydney Institute of Criminology, University of Sydney, p. 90; Haebich, A. 2000, *Broken circles: fragmenting Indigenous families 1800–2000*, Fremantle Arts Centre Press, Fremantle, p. 314; *Bringing them home: report of the national inquiry into the separation of Aboriginal and Torres Strait Island children from their families*, April 1997, p. 256.
10 Buti 2004, p. 23.
11 Penhall to Freda Brown, Bronte, NSW, 1 November 1951, GRG 52/1/1951/30.
12 Penhall to Mrs Geoff Thomas, 20 September 1941, GRG 52/1/1941/9.
13 Penhall to Mrs Wyld, 20 September 1941, GRG 52/1/1941/9.
14 See Roder, A.F. 1987, 'Aboriginal children under the law: a history of the specific legislative provisions relating to Aboriginal children in South Australia 1836–1972, Honours Thesis, University of Adelaide, p. 59.
15 Penhall to Chinnery, Director, Native Affairs, Darwin, 8 November 1939, GRG 52/8.
16 Peel to Penhall, 2 July 40, GRG 52/1/1940/14.
17 Penhall to Peel, 4 July 40, GRG 52/1/1940/14.
18 Peel to Penhall, 5 July 40, GRG 52/1/1940/14.
19 A.B. Erskine, Secretary, UAM, to Minister of Public Works, 10 September 1942, GRG 52/1/1941/81.
20 A.B. Erskine, Secretary, UAM, to Minister of Public Works, 10 September 1942, GRG 52/1/1941/81.
21 Penhall to Castine, 9 April 1943, GRG 52/1/1943/1.
22 Reverend G.A. Wood to Penhall, 4 November 1940, GRG 52/1/1940/44.
23 Penhall to Wood, 7 November 1940, GRG 52/1/1940/44.
24 South Australia, House of Assembly 1941, Debates, vol. 1, p. 851.
25 Duguid, 'Swan Reach, 30.6.40', GRG 52/1/1940/110.
26 Penhall to A. Wyld, Port Augusta, 16 October 1940, GRG 52/1/1940/9A.
27 South Australia, Parliament 1966, Representation by Cleland to Select Committee on Aboriginal Lands Trust Bill, Minutes of Evidence, 12 October 1966, GRG 52/24.
28 Cleland, J.B. 1965, 'Aborigines and land tenure', *Australian Journal of Science*, vol. 28, no. 1, pp. 164–165.
29 Anderson, W. 2002, *The cultivation of whiteness: science, health and racial destiny in Australia*, Melbourne University Press, Carlton, Victoria, p. 202.
30 Cleland, 'Impressions of a visit to Point McLeay', of 1 May 1940, GRG 52/1/1940/93
31 See, for instance, Penhall to OIC, Berri Police Station, 4 March 1941, GRG 52/1/1941/2, where Penhall requested of the Berri police that they warn a particular Aboriginal man that unless he contributed money towards his children's maintenance at Point McLeay, they would be made wards of the state.
32 Penhall to Scott Winter, Meningie, 19 March 1942, GRG 52/1/1940/39.

33 Penhall to APB, 1 May 1942, GRG 52/1/1940/39.

34 Penhall to M. Shepherd, 23 April 1941, GRG 52/1/1941/1.

35 Penhall to Piage, 4 July 1941, GRG 52/1/1941/6.

36 Penhall to A. Wyld, Umeewarra Mission, 17 May 1941, GRG 52/1/1941/9.

37 GRG 52/1/1941/10.

38 *The News*, Tuesday, 9 December 1941, p. 3.

39 GRG 52/1/1942/1.

40 Molony, J. 1987, *The Penguin bicentennial history of Australia: the story of 200 years*, Viking, Ringwood, Victoria, p. 287.

41 Gibbs 1984, p. 218.

42 Fort, C.S. 1996, '"Equality of sacrifice?": war work in Salisbury, South Australia', in *Playford's South Australia: essays on the history of South Australia 1933–1968*, Association of Professional Historians Inc, Adelaide, p. 217.

43 Roder, 1987, p. 77.

44 Penhall to Mrs Beryl Gardner, Quorn, 7 October 1942, GRG 52/1/1942/7.

45 Penhall to Eaton, 7 October 1942, GRG 52/1/1942/7.

46 Penhall to Wright, Warrakimba Station, 2 March 1943, GRG 52/1/1943/12.

47 Penhall to Commissioner of Public Works, 19 July 1943, GRG 52/1/1941/88.

48 Connell to Penhall, 5 August 1942, GRG 52/1/1941/7.

49 Penhall to Connell, 28 September 1942, GRG 52/1/1941/7.

50 McKenzie to Secretary, Aborigines Protection Board, re visit to Point McLeay Station of 15 May 1944, GRG 52/1/1944/33.

51 Penhall to OIC, Meningie Police Station, 24 May 1944, GRG 52/1/1944/33.

52 Mounted Constable McInerney, Meningie Police Station to Penhall, 27 May 1944, GRG 52/1/1944/33.

53 Mounted Constable McInerney, Meningie Police Station, to Penhall, 27 May 1944, GRG 52/1/1944/33.

54 McKenzie to Secretary, Aborigines Protection Board, re Wudinna, 16 June 1944, GRG 52/1/1944/33.

55 Penhall to OIC, Wudinna Police Station, 30 June 1944, GRG 52/1/1944/33.

56 Veitch, Wudinna Police Station to Penhall, 17 July 1944, GRG 52/1/1944/33.

57 GRG 52/1/1944/59.

58 Payne to Penhall, 19 July 1943, GRG 52/1/1943/9.

59 Penhall to OIC, Meningie Police Station, 23 July 1943, GRG 52/1/1943/9.

60 OIC, Meningie Police Station, to Penhall, 26 July 1943, GRG 52/1/1943/9.

61 *The News*, Tuesday 20 July 1943, p. 2.

62 Bolton, G. 1990, The *Oxford history of Australia, volume 5, 1942–1988: the middle way*, Oxford University Press, Melbourne, p. 29.

63 Penhall to Minister of Works, 21 June 1949, GRG 52/1/1949/58.

64 Penhall to Mr G. Stevenson, Pascoe Vale, Victoria, 28 June 1943, GRG 52/1/1943/18.

65 South Australia, House of Assembly 1942, Debates, vol. 1, p. 101.

66 Penhall to Aborigines Protection Board, 16 December 1943, GRG 52/1/1940/97.

67 Penhall to Kathleen Grimmett, 16 February 1944, GRG 52/1/1944/11.

68 GRG 52/1/1944/11.

69 South, Secretary to Commissioner of Public Works, to Frank Reid, 3 May 1944, GRG 52/1/1944/2.

70 Penhall to Peter McCormack, Morphett Vale, 25 May 1944, GRG 52/1/1943/80.

71 Erskine to Penhall, 1 August 1944, GRG 52/1/1943/80.
72 Penhall to Aborigines Protection Board, 15 August 1944, GRG 52/1/1943/80.
73 Penhall to McCormack, 16 August 1944, GRG 52/1/1943/80.
74 Erskine to Penhall, 2 February 1945, GRG 52/1/1943/80.
75 Kartinyeri, D. 2000, *Kick the tin*, Spinifex Press, North Melbourne, p. 9.
76 GRG 52/1/1946/59.
77 Penhall to Minister of Works, 22 November 1946, GRG 52/1/1946/59.
78 Hannan, Crown Solicitor, to the Attorney-General, 13 December 1946, GRG 52/1/1946/59.
79 Penhall to Secretary, UAM, 18 November 1946, GRG 52/1/1946/59.
80 Penhall to Minister of Works, 4 June 1946, GRG 52/1/1946/31.
81 Penhall to Minister of Works, 4 June 1946, GRG 52/1/1946/31.

CHAPTER FOUR

All natives are liars, 1946–1949

1 Penhall to the Acting Secretary, Aborigines Welfare Board, Chief Secretary's Office, Sydney, 1 September 1944, GRG 52/1/1944/18.
2 Penhall to the Acting Secretary, Aborigines Welfare Board, Chief Secretary's Office, Sydney, 1 September 1944, GRG 52/1/1944/18.
3 Pearce to Penhall, 14 October 1946, GRG 52/1/1946/18.
4 Penhall to Pearce, 25 October 1946, GRG 52/1/1946/18.
5 Penhall to Mr F.K. Smith, McLaren Vale, 28 November 1947, GRG 52/1/1947/30.
6 Penhall to Dr E.J. Davies, Malekula, New Hebrides, 14 August 1945, GRG 52/1/1945/3.
7 Penhall to Police Officer Fitzgerald, Wudinna, 15 April 1946, GRG 52/1/1946/52.
8 Acting Secretary Bray, to Manager, Point McLeay Station, 16 January 1947, GRG 52/1/1947/2.
9 Penhall to Professor Elkin, University of Sydney, 20 September 1950, GRG 52/1/1950/27.
10 GRG 52/1/1943/10.
11 Davies, Report, July 1943, GRG 52/1/1943/102.
12 Davies, Report, July 1943, GRG 52/1/1943/102.
13 See GRG 52/1/1944/33.
14 Kartinyeri, D. 2000, pp. xiii-xvi.
15 McKenzie to Bartlett, Point McLeay Station, 18 July 1947, GRG 52/1/1947/16.
16 Personal communication, Dr Rita Horwitz, January 2003.
17 GRG 52/1/1951/98.
18 Penhall to OIC, Port Germein Police Station, 31/7/47, GRG 52/1/1947/45.
19 *Advertiser*, 18 February 1947.
20 Penhall to Minister of Works, 15 July 1946, GRG 52/1/1945/45-46 [At end of 1946 files].
21 Penhall to Minister of Works, 15 July 1946, GRG 52/1/1945/45-46 [At end of 1946 files].
22 Acting Secretary Bray to Minister of Works, 23 January 1947, GRG 52/1/1947/3.
23 Penhall to Minister of Works, 14 May 1947, GRG 52/1/1947/66.
24 Penhall to Minister of Works for the Premier, 14 August 1947, GRG 52/1/1947/12.
25 P.W. Beckenham, Headmaster, Central School, Stroud, NSW, to Penhall, 24 May 1946, GRG 52/1/1946/22.
26 Penhall to Beckenham, 13 June 1946, GRG 52/1/1946/22.

27 Penhall to Beckenham, 13 June 1946, GRG 52/1/1946/22.

28 Miss A. Hollidge, Aborigines Advancement League, to Superintendent Point Pearce Station, 23 October 1947, GRG 52/1/1947/1C.

29 Bray to Manager, Point Pearce Station, 31 October 1947, GRG 52/1/1947/1C.

30 In contrast to the secrecy which pervaded the administration of Aboriginal affairs under Penhall, A.O. Neville, the Protector of Aborigines in Western Australia, reacted to government inaction there in the mid 1920s by *publicising* the plight of his Aboriginal charges. He embarked on a campaign of letter and article writing and lectures to service associations and church groups, all aimed at creating public awareness of Aboriginal deprivation. See Jacobs, P. 1990, *Mr Neville: a biography*, Fremantle Arts Centre Press, Fremantle, p. 128.

31 In December 1946, there occurred a very rare case of Cleland, as the acting Chairman of the Board, amending one of Penhall's recommendations prior to it being approved. Cleland made it clear that an Aboriginal man, whom Penhall had recommended be allowed to return to Point McLeay Station for Christmas, was not to leave his employment and return to the Station permanently (see Penhall to Aborigines Protection Board, 18 December 1946, GRG 52/1/1946/39A). It was a minor amendment, as it is clear that there was no intention on Penhall's part to allow such a thing to happen.

32 Penhall to Minister of Works, 14 May 1947, GRG 52/1/1947/66.

33 Cleland, 11 August 1947, GRG 52/1/1947/66.

34 Anderson 2002, p. 227.

35 Thomas, D. 2004, *Reading doctor's writing: race, politics and power in Indigenous health research, 1870–1969*, Australian Institute of Aboriginal and Torres Strait Islander Studies, Canberra, p. 70.

36 E.P. Southwell, Gerard Mission, to Penhall, 9 July 1947, GRG 52/1/1947/23.

37 Penhall to Aborigines Protection Board, 2 September 1947, GRG 52/1/1947/23.

38 Andrea Grant, Swan Reach to Penhall, 19 June 1945, GRG 52/1/1945/61.

39 Penhall to Grant, 23 June 1945, GRG 52/1/1945/61.

40 McKenzie, 'Port Augusta, 28/10/47', GRG 52/1/1947/53A.

41 Penhall to Miss Simmons, 7 November 1947, GRG 52/1/1947/53A.

42 Simmons to Penhall, 2 December 1947, GRG 52/1/1947/53A.

43 GRG 52/14, 2 January 1948.

44 McKenzie, 'Port Augusta, 12/1/48', GRG 52/1/1947/53A.

45 Penhall to Manager, Point Pearce Station, 28 November 1947, GRG 52/1/1947/16.

46 T.F. Matthews to Penhall, 10 February 1948, 52/1/1948/3.

47 Penhall to Matthews, 11 February 1948, 52/1/1948/3.

48 Bartlett to Penhall, 22 February 1945, GRG 52/1/1945/37.

49 McKenzie to Secretary, Children's Welfare and Public Relief Department, 6 May 1952, GRG 52/1/1952/3.

50 Penhall to Manager, Point Pearce Station, 4 December 1947, GRG 52/1/1947/53A.

51 Penhall to Chairman, CWPRB, 5 December 1947, GRG 52/1/1947/44.

52 Penhall, undated, GRG 52/1/1947/50.

53 Chairman, CWPRB, to Penhall, 15 December 1947, GRG 52/1/1947/44. In August 2004, I was informed by the Department for Family and Community Services that my December 2003 application to access GRG 29/6 (the correspondence files of the Children's Welfare and Public Relief Department) could not be granted. This record group could shed further light on the contrasting approaches to Aboriginal custody and guardianship taken by the welfare authorities and the Aborigines Department in South Australia.

54 Walloscheck to Penhall, 29 January 1948, GRG 52/1/1948/1.

55 GRG 52/14, 1948 diary.
56 Walloscheck to Penhall, 24 February 1948, GRG 52/1/1948/1; GRG 52/1/1948/1A, p. 37.
57 Carol Anderson to Penhall, 24 February 1948, GRG 52/1/1948/1.
58 Penhall to Walloscheck, 27 February 1948, GRG 52/1/1948/1.
59 See GRG 52/1/1945/45.
60 GRG 52/14, 19 January 1948.
61 Mrs Mary Reid to Penhall, 22 January 1948, GRG 52/1/1948/46.
62 Penhall to Aborigines Protection Board, 28 January 1948, GRG 52/1/1948/46.
63 Penhall to Bartlett, 3 September 1948, GRG 52/1/1948/2A.
64 Simmons to Penhall, 11 February 1948, GRG 52/1/1948/44.
65 Penhall to Simmons, 12 February 1948, GRG 52/1/1948/44.
66 Bolton, 1990, p. 61.
67 Bolton, 1990, p. 62.
68 Bolton, 1990, p. 61.
69 Penhall to Minister of Works, 2 December 1948, GRG 52/1/1940/102.
70 GRG 52/1/1949/3A.
71 GRG 52/1/1949/17.
72 GRG 52/1/1949/25.
73 GRG 52/1/1948/3.
74 Penhall to Director of Agriculture, 19 July 1948, GRG 52/1/1948/3.
75 Penhall to Mrs Burnard, 7 June 1950, GRG 52/1/1950/2.
76 Barbara Miller, Rose Park, to Penhall, 15 July 1950, GRG 52/1/1950/3A.
77 Penhall to Miller, 17 July 1950, GRG 52/1/1950/3A.
78 Miller to Penhall, 31 July 1950, GRG 52/1/1950/3A.
79 Penhall to Commissioner of Police, 18 February 1949, GRG 52/1/1949/50.
81 Penhall to Commissioner of Police, 30 March 1949, GRG 52/1/1949/70.
81 Walloscheck to Penhall, 30 April 1949, GRG 52/1/1949/65.
82 Penhall to Walloscheck, 11 May 1949, GRG 52/1/1949/65.
83 GRG 52/1/1950/25.

CHAPTER FIVE

If it would be a punishment, 1949–1953

1 See e.g. GRG 52/1/1950/4; and Penhall to Secretary, UAM, 18 November 1948, GRG 52/1/1946/59.
2 Penhall to Walloscheck, Manager, Point Pearce Station, 7 January 1949, GRG 52/1/1949/1.
3 Carol Anderson, Port Augusta, to Penhall, February 1949, GRG 52/1/1949/50.
4 Penhall to Carol Anderson, 17 February 1949, GRG 52/1/1949/50.
5 Penhall to Simmons, 28 February 1949, GRG 52/1/1949/50.
6 Simmons to Penhall, 25 February 1949, GRG 52/1/1949/50.
7 See e.g. Hospital report, January 1949, GRG 52/1/1949/52.
8 Penhall's 'Interim Report by the Secretary of the Board, 6.4.1949', GRG 52/1/1949/58.
9 Penhall to Samuels, 16 May 1949, GRG 52/1/1949/64.
10 Penhall to Samuels, 16 May 1949, GRG 52/1/1949/64.

11 McKenzie, Report, Point McLeay Station, 19 September 1949, GRG 52/1/1949/65.

12 Mrs Mary Reid to Penhall, 13 October 1949, GRG 52/1/1949/2B.

13 Penhall to Bartlett, 25 October 1949, GRG 52/1/1949/2A.

14 Bartlett to Penhall, 6 December 1949, GRG 52/1/1949/2B.

15 Penhall to Bartlett, 9 December 1949, GRG 52/1/1949/2B.

16 Copy of Statement from Southwell, 12 April 1949, GRG 52/1/1949/25.

17 Penhall to General Secretary, UAM, 13 April 1949, GRG 52/1/1949/25.

18 Penhall to Minister of Works, 27 May 1949, GRG 52/1/1949/80.

19 Hannan, Crown Solicitor, to the Secretary, Attorney-General, 25 July 1949, GRG 52/1/1949/80. I have not been able to check the exact wording of this communication as this is one of the files that the Attorney-General has refused to allow me to access.

20 It may be that an unwritten or unfiled communication took place between Penhall and the Crown Solicitor on this matter. Something similar seems to have taken place in November 1949, when Penhall advised the Secretary of the Narrung Progress Association that no compensation would be forthcoming for a Mr Becker, whose house was broken into and set on fire by children from Point McLeay, because 'the Crown Solicitor has advised that the Board is not legally responsible for the action of these children' (Penhall to A.P. McNicol, 9 December 1949, GRG 52/1/1949/2B). There is, however, nothing in writing from the Crown Solicitor on this matter.

21 Penhall to Freda Brown, Bronte, NSW, 1 November 1951, GRG 52/1/1951/30.

22 McKenzie, Report, Berri and Gerard, 21 June 1949, GRG 52/1/1949/65.

23 Southwell to Penhall, 25 June 1949, GRG 52/1/1949/25.

24 Penhall to Aborigines Protection Board, 6 July 1949, GRG 52/1/1949/64.

25 Penhall to Andrea Grant, 7 July 1949, GRG 52/1/1949/64.

26 Southwell to Penhall, 14 July 1949, GRG 52/1/1949/25.

27 Penhall to Southwell, 20 July 1949, GRG 52/1/1949/25.

28 Southwell to Penhall, 1 August 1949, GRG 52/1/1949/25.

29 Penhall to Southwell, 5 August 1949, GRG 52/1/1949/25.

30 Penhall, 'Suggestions for the consideration by the Board of matters arising from the report of the Secretary following a visit to the Eastern States', GRG 52/1/1949/28.

31 See 'Admission of children to Aboriginal Institutions, etc', GRG 52/1/1949/65.

32 Secretary, Minister of Works, to Penhall, 29 March 1949, GRG 52/1/1949/3.

33 Penhall to Secretary, Minister of Works, 30 March 1949, GRG 52/1/1949/3.

34 Stock, J.T. 1996, 'The "Playmander": its origins, operation and effect on South Australia' in B. O'Neil, J. Raftery and K. Round (eds) *Playford's South Australia: essays on the history of South Australia, 1933–1986*, Association of Professional Historians, Inc., Adelaide, p. 83.

35 Ibid., 1996, p. 84.

36 Penhall to Minister of Works, 21 June 1949, GRG 52/1/1949/58.

37 Mrs Tim Reid, Point McLeay Station, to Penhall, 29 November 1950, GRG 52/1/1950/4.

38 Penhall to Aborigines Protection Board, 6 December 1950, GRG 52/1/1950/4.

39 McKenzie to Penhall, 'Point McLeay, 22-1-1951', GRG 52/1/1951/63.

40 Penhall to Simmons, 4 January 1950, GRG 52/1/1950/53.

41 Penhall to Simmons, 4 January 1950, GRG 52/1/1950/53.

42 'Interim Report by Secretary of the Board, Meeting 8.2.1950', GRG 52/1/1950/57.

43 McKenzie, Report, Port Augusta, 6 March 1950, GRG 52/1/1950/61.

44 Mrs Alison Hurst, Port Augusta, to Penhall, 24 May 1950, GRG 52/1/1950/53.

45 McKenzie, Report, Port Augusta, 30 May 1950, GRG 52/1/1950/61.

46 McKenzie to Craig Hurst, c/Simmons, Umeewarra Mission, 16 October 1950, GRG 52/1/1950/53.
47 GRG 52/1/1952/11, p. 22.
48 Samuels, General Secretary, UAM, to Penhall, 14 May 1951, GRG 52/1/1951/4.
49 Penhall to Aborigines Protection Board, 16 May 1951, GRG 52/1/1951/4.
50 Jill Taylor, Winkie, to Penhall, 16 April 1952, GRG 52/1/1951/4.
51 Penhall to Jill Taylor, 23 April 1952, GRG 52/1/1951/4.
52 McKenzie to Mrs W.D. French, Pernatty Station (via Port Augusta), 17 June 1953, GRG 52/1/1953/13.
53 Penhall to Kneebone, 31 March 1952, GRG 52/1/1952/3.
54 Penhall to Secretary, Minister of Works, 22 January 1953, GRG 52/1/1953/3.
55 Penhall to Secretary, Minister of Works, 25 May 1953, GRG 52/1/1953/3.
56 See e.g. GRG 52/1/1941/22, p. 67; Penhall to Mrs Rose Walsh, 5 June 1941, GRG 52/1/1941/26.
57 GRG 52/1/1953/3, p. 32.
58 GRG 52/1/1953/3, p. 25.
59 *The News*, 18 August 1953, p. 5.

CHAPTER SIX

Our girls for slaves: Koonibba Mission, 1936–1952

1 Brock, P. 1993, *Outback ghettos: A history of Aboriginal institutionalisation and survival*, Cambridge University Press, Melbourne, p. 66. Chapter 6
2 Ibid., p. 67.
3 Ibid., p. 68.
4 See Mattingley and Hampton, 1988, p. 204, who refer to GRG 52/1/1915/39.
5 M. Lawson to Chief Protector McLean, 2 January 1936, GRG 52/1/1936/3.
6 GRG 52/1/1936/3.
7 McLean to Superintendent, Koonibba, 4 January 1936, GRG 52/1/1936/3.
8 Traeger to Chief Protector, August 1936, GRG 52/1/1936/3.
9 Traeger to Chief Protector, August 1936, GRG 52/1/1936/3.
10 Chief Protector to Superintendent, Koonibba, 9 June 1938, GRG 52/1/1939/36.
11 Chief Protector to Superintendent, Point Pearce Station, 20 June 1938, GRG 52/1/1939/36.
12 Bray, Point Pearce Station, to Chief Protector, 24 June 1938, GRG 52/1/1939/36.
13 R.K. Traeger, Koonibba, to Chief Protector, received 27 June 1938, GRG 52/1/1939/36.
14 Chief Protector to Superintendent, Koonibba, 1 July 1938, GRG 52/1/1939/36.
15 Grace Sampson to Penhall, 14 November 1938, GRG 52/1/1939/36.
16 Chief Protector to Superintendent, Koonibba, 16 November 1938, GRG 52/1/1939/36.
17 C. Hoff to Chief Protector, 26 May 1939, GRG 52/1/1939/36.
18 Chief Protector to Hoff, 30 May 1939, GRG 52/1/1939/36.
19 Chief Protector to Mrs Sampson, 30 May 1939, GRG 52/1/1939/36.
20 Chief Protector to Mrs Sampson, 23 October 1939, GRG 52/1/1939/36.
21 Mrs Sampson to Chief Protector, 11 December 1939, GRG 52/1/1939/36.
22 Chief Protector to Mrs Sampson, 13 December 1939, GRG 52/1/1939/36.
23 Penhall, note, GRG 52/1/1939/71.

24 Mrs Josephine King, Koonibba, to Penhall, received 19 August 1939, GRG 52/1/1939/71.
25 Ibid.
26 Ibid.
27 Ibid.
28 Ibid.
29 Ibid.
30 Ibid.
31 Penhall, note, GRG 52/1/1939/71.
32 Mrs Josephine King to Penhall, 14 December 1939, GRG 52/1/1939/71.
33 Chief Protector to Mrs King, 22 December 1939, GRG 52/1/1939/71.
34 Mrs Josephine King to Chief Protector, 14 December 1939, GRG 52/1/1939/71.
35 Penhall to Aborigines Protection Board, GRG 52/1/1939/36.
36 Mrs Sampson to Board of Control (ie Aborigines Protection Board), 16 March 1940, GRG 52/1/1939/36.
37 Mrs Sampson to Penhall, 8 April 1940, GRG 52/1/1939/36.
38 Carol Wilkinson to Penhall, 23 May 1940, GRG 52/1/1940/16.
39 Penhall to Mrs Carol Wilkinson, 24 June 1940, GRG 52/1/1940/16; see also Traeger to Penhall, 6 June 1940, GRG 52/1/1940/16.
40 Harms, E. and Hoff, C. (eds) 1951, *Second Koonibba jubilee booklet, 1901–1951*, Hunkin, Ellis & King, Adelaide, p. 31.
41 Penhall, note, 8 July 1940, GRG 52/1/1939/36.
42 Traeger to Penhall, 9 October 1940, GRG 52/1/1940/16A.
43 Penhall to Traeger, 14 October 1940, GRG 52/1/1940/16A.
44 Traeger to Secretary, Aborigines Protection Board, 19 December 1940, GRG 52/1/1939/36.
45 Penhall to Aborigines Protection Board, 2 January 1941, GRG 52/1/1939/36.
46 Penhall to Traeger, 9 January 1941, GRG 52/1/1939/36.
47 Traeger to Secretary, Aborigines Protection Board, 29 January 1941, GRG 52/1/1939/36.
48 Deborah Doyle, Koonibba, to Penhall, 8 January 1941, GRG 52/1/1941/3.
49 Traeger to Penhall, 29 January 1941, GRG 52/1/1941/3.
50 Penhall to Doyle, 3 February 1941, GRG 52/1/1941/3.
51 Penhall to Traeger, 24 February 1941, GRG 52/1/1941/3.
52 Penhall to Harms, 24 July 1941, GRG 52/1/1941/3.
53 Penhall to Traeger, 4 August 1941, GRG 52/1/1941/3.
54 Penhall to Aborigines Protection Board, 5 August 1941, GRG 52/1/1941/3.
55 Traeger to Penhall, 29 January 1942, GRG 52/1/1942/10.
56 Penhall to Marielena Kennedy, 2 February 1942, GRG 52/1/1942/10.
57 Mrs Joyce Webb to Penhall, 2 July 1942, GRG 52/1/1942/10A.
58 Traeger to Penhall, 5 August 1942, GRG 52/1/1942/10A.
59 Penhall to Mrs Joyce Webb, 11 August 1942, GRG 52/1/1942/10A.
60 Traeger to Penhall, 23 December 1943, GRG 52/1/1943/10.
61 Ibid.
62 Penhall to Shaw, 28 December 1943, GRG 52/1/1943/10; Penhall to Reynolds, 28 December 1943, GRG 52/1/1943/10.
63 Penhall to Traeger, 4 January 1944, GRG 52/1/1943/10.
64 McKenzie to Secretary, Aborigines Protection Board, GRG 52/1/1944/33.
65 Traeger to Penhall, 12 October 1944, GRG 52/1/1944/10.

66 McKenzie to Secretary, Aborigines Protection Board, 14 March 1944, GRG 52/1/1944/33.
67 Traeger to Penhall, 5 April 1944, GRG 52/1/1944/33.
68 Penhall to Manager, Point Pearce Station, 27 April 1944, GRG 52/1/1944/33.
69 See, e.g. Mrs Taylor to Penhall, 18 May 1944, GRG 52/1/1944/10.
70 Traeger to Penhall, 6 June 1944, GRG 52/1/1944/10.
71 Harms and Hoff 1951, p. 31.
72 Penhall to Traeger, 8 November 1944, GRG 52/1/1944/10a.
73 GRG 52/1/1944/10a.
74 Traeger to Penhall, 13 July 1944, GRG 52/1/1944/59, Annual Report.
75 Traeger to Deputy Commissioner of Child Endowment, 6 June 1944, GRG 52/1/1944/33.
76 Traeger to Deputy Commissioner of Child Endowment, 6 June 1944, GRG 52/1/1944/33.
77 McKenzie to Secretary, Aborigines Protection Board, re Wudinna, 16 June 1944, GRG 52/1/1944/33.
78 Penhall to OIC, Wudinna Police Station, 30 June 1944, GRG 52/1/1944/33.
79 Traeger to Deputy Commissioner of Child Endowment, 6 June 1944, GRG 52/1/1944/33.
80 McKenzie to Secretary, Aborigines Protection Board, re Wudinna, 16 June 1944, GRG 52/1/1944/33.
81 Penhall to Traeger, 30 June 1944, GRG 52/1/1944/33.
82 Ibid.
83 Traeger to Penhall, 13 July 1944, GRG 52/1/1944/33.
84 Judy Lawson to Penhall, 9 August 1944, GRG 52/1/1944/10.
85 Traeger to Penhall, 30 August 1944, GRG 52/1/1944/10.
86 Ibid.
87 M. Lawson to Penhall, 31 August 1944, GRG 52/1/1944/10; M. Lawson to Penhall, 14 September 1944, GRG 52/1/1944/10.
88 Traeger to Penhall, 4 October 1944, GRG 52/1/1944/10.
89 Lawson to Penhall, 19 October 1944, GRG 52/1/1944/10.
90 Traeger to Penhall, 18 January 1945, GRG 52/1/1945/18.
91 Traeger to Penhall, 26 July 1945, GRG 52/1/1945/18a.
92 McKenzie to Secretary, Aborigines Protection Board, GRG 52/1/1945/54a.
93 Penhall to Traeger, 28 August 1945, GRG 52/1/1945/54a.
94 May 1946, GRG 52/1/1946/9.
95 Harms to Penhall, 1 May 1946, GRG 52/1/1946/25.
96 Traeger, Chapple St, Broken Hill, to Penhall, 2 December 1946, GRG 52/1/1946/25.
97 Penhall to Traeger, 6 December 1946, GRG 52/1/1946/25.
98 Eckermann to Penhall, 19 December 1946, GRG 52/1/1946/25.
99 C.V. Eckermann to Acting Secretary Bray, 27 December 1946, GRG 52/1/1947/28.
100 Eckermann, Koonibba, to Penhall, 24 January 1948, GRG 52/1/1948/20A.
101 Eckermann to Penhall, 3 May 1948, GRG 52/1/1948/28.
102 Penhall to Aborigines Protection Board, 5 May 1948, GRG 52/1/1948/20A.
103 Eckermann to Penhall, 27 May 1948, GRG 52/1/1948/58.
104 Penhall to Aborigines Protection Board, 11 August 1948, GRG 52/1/1948/28.
105 Eckermann to Penhall, 22 September 1948, GRG 52/1/1948/28.
106 Penhall to Eckermann, 27 September 1948, GRG 52/1/1948/28.
107 Eckermann to Penhall, 9 July 1952, GRG 52/1/1952/25.
108 Mrs Josephine King, Koonibba, to Penhall, received 19 August 1939, GRG

CHAPTER SEVEN

Legally indefensible: Concluding remarks

1 Bolton, G. in Jacobs, P. 1990, p. 13.Chapter 7

2 Personal communication, Joanna Richardson.

3 Garnett to Commissioner of Public Works, 10 December 1924, GRG 52/1/1924/89.

4 Chief Protector to Superintendent, Point Pearce Station, 4 January 1926, GRG 52/1/1926/4.

5 Chief Protector to Roger Anderson, 25 March 1931, GRG 52/1/1930/40.

6 Penhall to Francis Barnes, 30 November 1951, GRG 52/1/1951/49.

7 Trevorrow v. State of South Australia (no. 5) (2007). SASC 285, para. 41.

8 Penhall to Bourke, 17 August 1944, GRG 52/1/1944/59.

9 Berndt, R.M., Berndt, C.H. and Stanton, J.E. 1993, *A world that was: the Yaraldi of the Murray River and the lakes, South Australia*, Melbourne University Press, Carlton, p. 7.

10 Ibid., p. 7.

11 Rowe, G. 1959, *A century of service to the Aborigines at Point McLeay, South Australia*, reprinted from the 101st annual report of the Aborigines Friends Association, Aborigines Friends Association, Adelaide.

BIBLIOGRAPHY

Archival Sources

GRG 52/1	Aborigines Department, Correspondence Files of the Aborigines Office and Successor Agencies, 1866–1968.
GRG 52/8	Aborigines Department, Protector of Aborigines, Letter book relating to the Northern Territory (copies of letters sent), 1927–1939.
GRG 52/14	Aborigines Department, Office Diaries of the Secretary of the Advisory Council of Aborigines and of the Aborigines Protection Board, 1923–1954.
GRG 52/24	Aborigines Department, File on the Aboriginal Lands Trust Bill, 1966.

Legislation

Aborigines Act 1934–1939
Aborigines (Training of Children) Act 1923
State Children Act 1895

Books, reports, etc

Anderson, W. 2002, *The cultivation of whiteness: science, health and racial destiny in Australia*, Melbourne University Press, Carlton, Victoria.

Berndt, R.M., Berndt, C.H. and Stanton, J.E. 1993, *A world that was: the Yaraldi of the Murray River and the lakes, South Australia*, Melbourne University Press, Carlton.

Bolton, G. 1990, *The Oxford history of Australia, volume 5, 1942–1988: the middle way*, Oxford University Press, Melbourne.

Bringing them home: report of the national inquiry into the separation of Aboriginal and Torres Strait Island children from their families, April 1997.

Brock, P. 1993, *Outback ghettos: a history of Aboriginal institutionalisation and survival*, Cambridge University Press, Melbourne.

Buti, A.D. 2004, *Separated: Aboriginal childhood separations and guardianship law*, Sydney Institute of Criminology, University of Sydney.

Cleland, J.B. 1965, 'Aborigines and land tenure', *Australian Journal of Science*, vol. 28, no. 1, pp. 164–165.

Cockburn, S. 1991, *Playford: benevolent despot*, Axiom Publishers, Kent Town, South Australia.

Dickey, B. 1986, *Rations, residence, resources: a history of social welfare in South Australia since 1836*, Wakefield Press, Adelaide.

Elkin, A.P. 1979, 'Aboriginal-European relations in Western Australia: an historical and personal record', in C.H. and R.M. Berndt (eds) *Aborigines of the west: their past and their present*, University of Western Australia Press, Perth.

Fort, C.S. 1996, '"Equality of sacrifice?": war work in Salisbury, South Australia', in *Playford's South Australia: essays on the history of South Australia 1933–1968*, Association of Professional Historians Inc, Adelaide.

Gibbs, R.M. 1984, *A history of South Australia: from colonial days to the present*, Southern Heritage, Blackwood, Adelaide.

Haebich, A. 2000, *Broken circles: fragmenting indigenous families 1800–2000*, Fremantle Arts Centre Press, Fremantle.

Harms, E. and Hoff, C. (eds) 1951, *Second Koonibba jubilee booklet, 1901–1951*, Hunkin, Ellis & King, Adelaide.

Howell, P.A. 1996, 'Playford, politics and parliament', in *Playford's South Australia: essays on the history of South Australia 1933–1968*, Association of Professional Historians Inc, Adelaide.

Jacobs, P. 1990, *Mr Neville: a biography*, Fremantle Arts Centre Press, Fremantle.

Kartinyeri, D. 2000, *Kick the tin*, Spinifex Press, North Melbourne.

Manne, R. 2004, 'Aboriginal child removal and the question of genocide, 1900–1940' in D. Moses (ed.) *Genocide and settler society: frontier violence and stolen Indigenous children in Australian history*, Berghahn Books, New York.

Mattingley, C. and Hampton, K. 1988, *Survival in our own land: 'Aboriginal' experiences in 'South Australia' since 1836*, Wakefield Press, Adelaide.

Molony, J. 1987, *The Penguin bicentennial history of Australia: the story of 200 years*, Viking, Ringwood, Victoria.

Roder, A.F. 1987, 'Aboriginal children under the law: a history of the specific legislative provisions relating to Aboriginal children in South Australia 1836–1972', Honours Thesis, University of Adelaide.

Rowe, G. 1959, *A century of service to the Aborigines at Point McLeay, South Australia*, reprinted from the 101st annual report of the Aborigines Friends Association, Aborigines Friends Association, Adelaide.

Thomas, D. 2004, *Reading doctors' writing: race, politics and power in Indigenous health research, 1870–1969*, Australian Institute of Aboriginal and Torres Strait Islander Studies, Canberra.

Stock, J.T. 1996, 'The "Playmander": its origins, operation and effect on South Australia' in B. O'Neil, J. Raftery and K. Round (eds) *Playford's South Australia: essays on the history of South Australia, 1933–1986*, Association of Professional Historians, Inc., Adelaide.

ACKNOWLEDGEMENTS

This study almost exclusively uses primary historical material from the South Australian government archives to present its case. Thanks to the wonderful staff of State Records of South Australia for their advice and help in accessing this material.

Thanks also to Doreen Kartinyeri and Rita Horwitz for telling me of their experiences with the Aborigines Department; to Harry Powell, Dr Tim Rowse, Dr David Ness, David Mortimer, Tim Taylor and Professor Robert Manne for commenting on early versions of the manuscript; to Joanna Richardson for her comments regarding legal aspects of this work; and to Kathy Sharrad, Bruce McClintock and Wallace McKitrick for their invaluable advice and editorial expertise.

For everything else, thanks to Tania Madigan.

INDEX

www.ingramcontent.com/pod-product-compliance
Ingram Content Group Australia Pty Ltd
76 Discovery Rd, Dandenong South VIC 3175, AU
AUHW020613010925
416023AU00003B/40

9 781862 548046